Your intentional life is not something you chose

It's something you create !! :)

CREATE AWESOME

Journaling Your Way to an Intentional Life

Douglas W. Bundock

FriesenPress

One Printers Way
Altona, MB R0G 0B0
Canada

www.friesenpress.com

Copyright © 2024 by Douglas W. Bundock
First Edition — 2024

All rights reserved.

No part of this publication may be reproduced in any form, or by any means, electronic or mechanical, including photocopying, recording, or any information browsing, storage, or retrieval system, without permission in writing from FriesenPress.

ISBN
978-1-03-832131-2 (Hardcover)
978-1-03-832130-5 (Paperback)
978-1-03-832132-9 (eBook)

1. SELF-HELP, JOURNALING

Distributed to the trade by The Ingram Book Company

This book is lovingly dedicated to my mom, who has impacted my life in countless positive ways.

She was my Number One Fan and Number One Supporter.

I miss you every day, Mom.

The better parts of you live on in me.

Table of Contents

Introduction	xi
Faith	1
Goals	15
Giving	31
Kindness	43
Gratitude	53
Passion	63
Confidence	77
Legacy	95
Conclusion	105
A Short Compendium of Awesome	109
Committing to Awesome	113
Reasons to **J**ournal	115
JUST FOR **T**ODAY	119
Create **A**wesome	121
About the Author	123

With a passion for life, family, business and, most importantly, relationships, Doug is someone you want to listen to. I've known him for over 15 years, and his optimism is contagious, his success is admirable, and his story is enticing.

Gina Pelligrini, Pelligrini Team Consulting

It's rare to find someone whose purpose in life is to help others uncover their potential instead of just their own. Doug has been doing just this for years in both his personal and corporate career. Let Doug help you reach your potential in life—let him show you the way to creating your awesome! Whether you're in a groove or stuck in a rut, Doug will help you unleash your potential in life by helping you create awesome. He's honed his skills for years and created a model that will help you feel better about the way you live your life.

Aaron Abrams, President, Molly Maid Canda

If you're looking for more awesome in your life, Doug Bundock can help. His intentional approach to journaling will unlock your creativity, give meaning to your musings, and help you explore the core tenets of a life well lived and deeply experienced. With poignant stories from his own personal and professional journey, Doug outlines a methodology and system for creating a daily journaling practice. With Doug as your guide and journaling as your practice, your next days can be your best days.

Joey Coleman, keynote speaker and bestselling author of Never Lose a Customer Again, and Never Lose an Employee Again

---

I have been fortunate to work with Doug for almost 20 years. He consistently brings positivity, kindness and professionalism to every interaction. Despite having many challenging times in our industry, Doug always lives his core values and "creates an awesome" for everyone in his path. His enthusiasm for life is infectious, and I deeply value the times that we share.

Lisa White, former Business Development Manager, Northbridge Insurance Company

---

Doug's journey with intentional journaling showcases the incredible power of daily reflection. He exemplifies how by committing to this simple yet profound practice, one can experience significant personal growth. His story is a testament to how journaling can foster clarity, self-awareness, and a deeper understanding of one's goals, leading to meaningful progress in all areas of life.

Arianna DiCiocco, Intellectual Capital Team, Strategic Coach®

Introduction

What is awesome? Where does it come from? Can I create awesome in my life? Can I create awesome in other people's lives? And if I can, what habits will lead me there?

When I started to ask myself those questions over a decade ago, I embarked on a different path, a more intentional one that improved my well-being, advanced my career, strengthened my relationships, and invited more awe, goodness, and joy into my life.

If you're picking up this book, you're exploring ways to find the tools to invite those experiences into *your* life. Day-to-day life has become more littered with distractions, making it difficult to be reflective and intentional about how you want to move through this world. Perhaps you feel like time is passing by, and you're not playing an active role in, or even paying attention to, your life. You are just existing. You may have realized that quick fixes are not the solution to persistent problems, and you want to explore strategies that will change the quality of your lifelong term.

You have come to the right place. This book outlines the tenets and tools I have used to build a more fulfilling and intentional life.

The global COVID-19 pandemic did a number on us all. Collectively, we were sad, angry, and confused. But it also forced us to slow down and simplify our days. Once we were alone with our thoughts, many of us reevaluated our lives, reflecting on where we were, where we wanted to be, and what changes would bring us more fulfillment. For the past decade, this kind of quiet reflection has been critical to answering the questions I opened with. But now, that involuntary period of quiet introspection is over, and we have returned to our hectic lives. How many of us have continued reflecting?

I doubt anyone wants to bring back a global pandemic to get some quiet time, and the good news is, we do not have to have a pandemic to get that introspective time back. We can maintain a practice of quiet reflection even though life is back to its normal busyness. We can all carve out some time every day to think, reflect, plan, and, in the process, make positive changes to our lives and relationships.

The human brain has roughly 60,000 thoughts a day, and 80 percent of those are negative. On top of that, the same negative thoughts re-occur every single day. How do we break the pattern? By creating good habits that rewire the brain to be more positive.

Those habits are simple: get quiet, listen, be aware, and then take time to write and reflect. Our thoughts are everything: good or bad, positive or negative, real or imagined. We become where our thoughts take us. Have you ever had a thought that leads to worry and anxiousness? The thought takes on a life of its own. Then, you later find that the thought and its corresponding anxiousness are just a figment of your imagination of unnecessary worry.

If our thoughts can dictate our decisions and behaviours, then it makes sense to control our thoughts. If we focus on negativity or perhaps sad stories in the news, what is the impact of those thoughts in the long term? They may cause you to wake up at night or even dream of situations. The mind is a powerful tool, and if we take the time to control the input, the output will also be maintained. We can create reflections that positively impact our lives through constant daily affirmation and journaling.

If you do not know where to start, do not worry. The eight tenets this book outlines give you an agenda or road map for creating new patterns that enable us to create awesome. Even if you only write a few sentences about one word each day, you will notice a difference in your well-being. These words have helped me move through life with clarity and purpose. I feel in control, and even when I am not in control, I do not panic or fret. I first take time to put events into perspective. Because of my continuous habit of positive reflection and planning, my mind goes first to positive rather than negative. We are to learn from all the events that take place from day to day in our lives. I have often said my superpower is my calmness. That is due to the habit of journaling using these tenets I am outlining here.

Why Bother Creating Awesome?

About twelve years ago, I attended a business seminar in Toronto put on by a company called The Art Of. On this particular day, the speaker started talking about awesome. Everything was awesome to him, from the smell of toast to freshly cleaned sheets. Before that day, I had always believed that the word awesome was overused. Afterward, however, I could not stop thinking about it. For the rest of that day, I repeatedly asked myself, "Not everything is awesome—or is it?" That day turned into a week, a month, a year, and soon, a decade. I kept wondering about awesome: *Where does awesome come from? How can we create awesome things for ourselves? How can we create awesome for other people?* I was looking for ways to encourage my team and our clients, so I integrated that question into my personal and business lives. I set a goal for myself and my team at our insurance office: create awesome with every phone call, email, or communication. We even put signs around the office to remind people to create awesome.

That is how it started. Those questions evolved into the eight tenets that I believe create awesome. These eight words influence my life more than others: Faith, Goals, Giving, Kindness, Gratitude, Passion, Confidence, and Legacy. The words themselves are only part of the answer. A daily habit of focusing and writing helps the words come to life.

I chose these tenets with great care because I know how important a single word can be. I also placed them in an order that consciously and thoughtfully builds toward creating awesome.

- **FAITH** is first because, for me, everything flows through faith. For the next seven tenets to truly work their magic, you must believe that journaling about them and incorporating them into your day will make a difference in your life. Faith is the foundation of my life, guiding all of the other words. There is spiritual faith, which I will get into later, and a confident faith in ourselves. They are different, but I believe as human beings, we require both to achieve the maximum potential in our lives.

- **GOALS** are next because you must set goals to achieve *anything*, including becoming more intentional, kinder, or confident.

- Sharing your gifts through **GIVING** is essential to living a complete life.

- **KINDNESS** is not only the Golden Rule in treating others; it's also a way to increase your capacity to deal with difficulties and challenges.

- **GRATITUDE** will help you recognize how full and rich your life already is.

- Finding and developing your **PASSION** will give you the energy to keep going and find that intentional life.

- **CONFIDENCE** is crucial to leading a successful life, so build grounded, unshakable self-confidence.

- Everyone, including you, can leave a **LEGACY** in their life. Legacy is last because it's how you will be thought of and remembered by your family, friends, loved ones, and community.

I believe that to live our richest, fullest life and to create more awesome; we must reflect on these words and concepts each day and then act on them.

To do that, I developed a journaling habit that integrates these words and this practice into my life. I will share my personal experiences with these eight tenets in every chapter. I will outline how journaling with these words improved my life. Each chapter ends with a journaling exercise to get you started so you can let these words change *your* life in new and different ways.

Get into a Good Habit

When it came to improving my life, forming good habits was where the rubber met the road. Committing to journaling practice helped me make active, affirming, and intentional choices. Now, each day, I journal, and I use these eight words to guide my heart and mind. I may write a sentence or an entire paragraph. I do not plan it; I just let it flow. That is what is great about journaling. There are no rules. Instead, you write from your heart and mind.

I do not know about you, but I can't write in a journal without coffee. I'm particular to Starbucks and even more fond of my daughter and son-in-law's brand, Lord & Lady Coffee Inc. (Yes, a shameless plug. I can do that; it's my book! www.lordandlady.ca). So, in the morning, I take some time—it could be forty-five minutes or more—to sit down, drink my coffee, and clear away distractions, such as my phone. (We are all so distracted by our phones that sometimes I hate them.) That way, it is just me and my thoughts. This quiet time of solitude is when I tap into who I am and devise more intentional plans for myself. Taking this time shows my life is not just about *existing* and *surviving*. During this daily quiet reflection, I am proactively *creating* my life.

Typically, I journal from seven to eight every morning. That is my sacred time. I will go to the coffee shop closest to my office and write for an hour. Carving out time to think, ponder, listen, and pray nourishes my soul and spirit. Every day can bring chaos, so this time sets the foundation for my day by creating a sense of calm and peacefulness.

Getting Quiet

When quiet, we delve into our soul and write about what matters. That is when we can address the tough questions. Many people do not like to journal because they'll have to acknowledge hurtful things that happened in the past or fears they have about the future. They may struggle to write about difficult childhood moments, painful relationships, persistent worries, or nagging regrets. Writing about these things can hurt, but it allows us to work through them. Most of us try to sweep these issues under the rug, either intentionally or subconsciously. Getting quiet will help us realize we need counselling or a better support system to resolve these issues. That may seem daunting, but these are the first steps to a better life. Most of us struggle with something. I'm no different.

My younger sister, Kathleen, passed away when she was only two. I was four then, and over the years, I watched how her death impacted my whole family. My parents each dealt with the loss differently. My mom chose to rise through her sorrow. She still addressed the pain that losing Kathleen caused her but also decided to have a joyful life in tandem with it. But my father never dealt with his grief. Instead, I believe he closed himself off to family and threw himself further into work and golf as a distraction. I saw firsthand how those differing reactions shaped my parents' lives. My mother's life seemed more fulfilled and connected, and my father's life seemed more distant and resigned.

The inability of my father to deal with all this emotion created a gulf in his life, and this caused issues in many areas, including our relationship. Because of this, it hurt me a lot. Still, as I got older and embarked on a ritual of journaling, I contemplated our relationship more fully. I put myself in my dad's shoes by quieting myself and working through these prompts and exercises. I wondered what it would feel like to lose a child and how I might cope. These exercises helped me process the complexity of that situation. After my father passed, I spent hours journaling and conversing with my mother about him. When I stepped back and reflected, I realized how much pain he was in. His aloof nature wasn't about me. Rather, my father was in pain and not coping well with losing his daughter, my sister. Unfortunately, my dad never learned how to manage this terrible loss in his life and never asked for help.

Journaling helped me to put all of this into perspective. I wish the overall relationship with my dad was deeper. Still, journaling allowed me to process the past and find a way forward. Moreover, I decided I wanted to be a different kind of father to my daughter, and journaling helped me achieve that goal. Writing out my thoughts and feelings helped me create the relationship I wanted with my daughter, Kristen. Understanding the negatives from prior relationships helped me correct my behaviour to ensure history did not repeat itself. I may never have allowed myself to embrace the situation and move on fully had I not taken the time to get quiet and journal.

I believe that inside us is everything we need, but we don't make the time to figure it out. It's hard, it's painful, and it takes time. Journaling has become a key component in achieving those goals. When obstacles or sad moments arise, I sit down, get quiet, and do the inner work to figure it out.

This practice has been instrumental to my mental health and well-being, so I designed the exercises in this book to help me, and now I'm sharing them with you. At the end of each chapter, you will find a set of journaling prompts that encourage making time for quiet reflection and surrounding yourself with a strong support system.

From Average to Awesome

I was born into a strict religious household with many rules, which I followed judiciously. I wasn't a big fan of school, but I made my way through primary and secondary school. Because I didn't connect with the party-heavy atmosphere of high school, I skipped university, which I knew would offer more of the same. Instead, I followed my father into the insurance business. While our relationship was sometimes distant, I learned much about insurance from my dad. He was an outstanding salesperson and brilliant with clients. He taught me to treat people with respect, honesty, and integrity—three key components to any business, especially in insurance.

About eight years after I started working with him, my dad decided to sell the business. Before he did, he asked if I wanted to take it over. I was still young and had no idea what I wanted to do long-term, so I told him to go ahead and sell. It was a difficult decision, but in the end, venturing from the family business was one of the best things that ever happened to me. I ended up staying in insurance, and over the next few years, I worked for different brokerages, which exposed me to innovative ideas and innovative leaders. From there, I quickly moved into a leadership role. When I did, I realized that being a servant was the true role of a leader. And so, during my nearly five-decade tenure in the insurance industry, being a servant leader has become a core value. Moving forward with that mentality, I steadily rose through the ranks. Now, I'm the Chief "Optimistic" Operating Officer of a $150 million brokerage with a hundred employees. I never had a goal to be a COO. I wanted to have a positive influence and to serve. Those two goals led me to this place.

I'm proud of my achievements, but this book is not about my work. I'm not here to tell you I'm perfect; I'm not that guy, and this isn't that book. I'm an average guy with his share of ups and downs. I graduated from Leaside High School in Toronto with average marks. I was an adequate athlete. I'm divorced with one amazing daughter and son-in-law with three grandkids. I have a significant other in Sara, and along the way, I've found journaling a useful tool to impact my life for the better. I have developed stronger relationships with my family, friends, and business community using this tool regularly. I have increased my philanthropy and have grown tenfold in my career. I have a sense of inner fulfillment and accomplishment. I am creating awesome.

When you write about your life through the lens of these eight tenets, a similar transformation will take place. Whatever your situation or life entails, you can work with it and find more fulfillment by adopting intentional journaling practices.

Over the years, I've learned that creating awesome in my life and the lives of others consists of small steps. It's not rocket science, but it does take a bit of focus and the willingness to develop good habits. Don't expect an overnight miracle. This method is a day-by-day journey. When you start, you won't know where you're going. That's okay. When I started thinking about awesome ten-plus years ago, I never dreamed I'd write a book. Yet here I am. That's the mystery. And the magic.

But your journey doesn't begin until you take that first step forward. So, let's start and take the next step together.

1

Faith

"Complete trust or confidence in someone or something."

You might think life becomes a cakewalk once you have spiritual faith. You've trusted something or someone, and now you can kick back and relax. But that couldn't be further from the truth. Your faith will be constantly tested. Mine certainly was after I separated from my wife of many years in 1996.

I grew up attending a Pentecostal church. The Pentecostal faith is quite strict. There is no drinking or dancing and certainly no cussing. Family and church life are central, and divorce is frowned upon. Growing up, I didn't go out to play or watch TV on Sundays. Instead, my family went to church twice, in the morning and again in the evening. We spent the remainder of the day at home. I carried these Pentecostal traditions and others into adulthood and marriage.

Before I was separated and then divorced, I was deeply involved with our local church. I was part of the social groups, attended meetings, and sang in choirs and many worship teams. But after our divorce, my church community ignored me; I no longer mattered to them. My mother, who adored my ex-wife, didn't speak to me for a year. After I moved out of the house and lived alone, my family never came to see my new place. Even worse, the separation weighed on my ten-year-old daughter. It was a painful season in my life. I went to work for many weeks, came home, and lay down in the dark. I barely ate. I didn't watch TV. I didn't do anything. I wasn't sure if I wanted to keep going.

I had already started questioning God before my divorce. Now, alone night after night, I questioned *everything* about life, especially my faith. Based on how I was brought up and taught in the church, I figured I had pretty much destroyed my life and my family's reputation. You see, the church I attended put so much emphasis on things that, in my opinion, are unimportant. I understand why some things like drinking and dancing were thought to be things that you should control because, if not controlled, they could cause you to be tempted to cross socially unacceptable lines. The levels of judgment were over the top, and still, to this day, I believe the amount of judgment that goes on is unacceptable. I found that when I started questioning my faith, it was not really about religion; it was about rules. Faith or belief is not about rules but God's love for us. At that moment, I understood, and God met me in my absolute worst place. God shows himself calmly and respectfully when we have nothing else to lean on. And slowly, leaning on my faith, I hiked out of the valley I was living in with God's help. I was battle-weary and bruised, but I was alive and ready to see what life had in store for me.

After faith delivered me through that dark period, I still had to rebuild my life. I was starting over in many ways but was still determining who I was and wanted to be. So, I spent the next ten years asking myself questions: *Doug, here's what you've been living, but here's what you've been thinking, and there's a big disconnect. Does it make sense to have an entire day devoted to being quiet? Does it make sense that you can never have a glass of wine with dinner or dance at a wedding?* Then, of course, the questions got bigger. *What is life? What are we here for? There's got to be more than what I'm experiencing.*

I did a lot of soul-searching and figured out what I deemed important. If we strive for perfection, we will live a life of frustration. All we need to do is try to be better today than yesterday. I figured out who Doug was and, more importantly, who Doug wanted to be. I had been living a certain life because of my upbringing; it was time to choose what made sense. At this point in my life, I had not started journaling or writing, but I wanted to dig deep, and I felt I needed to write things down to do that. For me, writing slows things down and brings them into focus.

I spent a decade walking through that dark uncertainty into the light, using my journal and a newfound sense of introspection. Working on myself led me to meet Sara, my partner, who I have been with for the past eighteen years. I also grew closer to my mother, Patricia Bundock, who remained my Number One Fan, friend, inspiration, and mentor until the last day of her life.

During my low points, if you had told me all the magical things my future held, I would have struggled to believe you. My conservative religious upbringing convinced me that my divorce had irreparably damaged my life . . . and yet, deep down, even in my darkest hour, I tenderly nurtured the faith that God had a plan for me. That turned out to be true. God meets us at our toughest times. When things are good, we tend to forget about God. But these days, having a daily journaling practice reminds me of God and His place in my life. God is the most important person in my life. Without Him, the rest does not matter.

From my divorce, I learned that many people fear God will hit them with lightning if they don't do everything right. I had long believed that God was done with me because I failed. But not anymore. God understands us. He knows that we are not perfect. He wants us to have a personal relationship with Him. He loves and wants the best for us, especially when we go through challenging times and make complex decisions.

In retrospect, I never questioned my faith in God or His plan. I challenged the church. I examined the organization that—as I saw it—counted heads in the pews and in the offering plate. I questioned the judgment of how former friends and community members were treating me. But I never actually lost faith in *God*. It was cloudy for a time, for sure, but my faith and God were there all the time. I know He'll always be there and is my stabilizing force. Faith has strengthened me because of its original early foundation in my life. When I thought it was gone or did not exist, it was hidden under much pain and disappointment. It has stuck with me, and I have it during my toughest and most uncertain times.

I believe that even if you feel like you have nowhere to turn, you do. You can turn to your faith. In this chapter, I'll share an experience that led me to find my faith, and I hope you will find yours and lean more deeply into it.

Letting Faith Take Over

My calling upon my faith has given me the confidence and strength to move forward through good times and bad. Faith means believing in a higher power and knowing I am part of a divine purpose without concrete proof. I am on Earth for a reason. They say that two days in your life are the most important: the day you are born, and the day you understand why.

Some people think faith is born out of ease, joy, and good times, but it's quite the opposite. Faith is often found in moments of pain, challenge, and doubt. I've experienced many personal, emotional, and professional peaks and valleys. Some of those valleys, like my divorce, have made me question everything. But after sixty-five-plus years of marching deep into those valleys, I've also trudged out, step by step, by leaning on my faith.

Faith is an *intentional, ongoing process*, not an outcome. Even now, after so much practice, having faith is *still* a process for me. I must take a moment every day—sometimes every hour—to build and nurture my faith.

Faith is unseen and intangible. We can't put our hands on it. So, in many ways, faith is the most difficult concept in this book. We want proof. We want to see, touch, and hold it in our hands. But faith is an invisible force that lives in the heart and the soul. And even more important, *faith is a decision*. We either decide to have faith or we don't. I know it can be hard to pin your hopes and dreams on something you can't hold on to, but I promise that letting things flow through faith will positively alter the course of your life. When you take time to journal, you allow God to speak to you—not out loud but to your spirit. He can bring situations to mind and guide your thoughts. It is journaling and being quiet and undistracted from our busy lives.

Faith showed up for me most simply and unexpectedly during the last moments of my father's life. My dad was healthy as a horse until he was about sixty-five. And then, within four short years, he had a hip replacement, a heart attack, and pancreatic cancer. Boom, boom, boom.

The cancer diagnosis came in October 1999. The whites of his eyes turned yellow, and initially, the doctors thought it was his gallbladder, but it was nothing too serious. It was around Halloween, so we kept joking that he didn't need a mask due to the strange color of his eyes. Then the test results came back, and it was Stage IV pancreatic cancer—a death sentence by all accounts. We knew what we were dealing with but hoped for more time together.

In early November 1999, shortly after his diagnosis, they took him in for surgery, and my mom, brother, and I all waited in the waiting room at the hospital. I remember looking down the hall about an hour into the surgery and seeing the doctor in the hallway. That wouldn't be good if he were already out of the operating room. I was right. Dad was so full of cancer that the surgeon closed him back up. They gave him about six months to live.

Over the next few months, my brother, mother, and I were in a steady rotation at our father's side. In the year he was in the hospital, my mom only missed one day seeing him. She still worked full time but made it in to see Dad on her way to work, and every evening, she stayed with him. On November 12, 2000, almost exactly a year after his first diagnosis, my mom and I visited Dad. It was a Sunday morning, and I'd come to stay with my mom for the weekend. By then, dad was pretty out of it and had been for the last month. He must have lost a hundred pounds since the diagnosis. The nurse came in and asked us to leave the room so she could change the sheets. My mom and I started to walk out, and as the nurse passed me, she turned around, grabbed my elbow, and said, "Don't go far."

Mom and I stepped into the hall. Thirty seconds later, the nurse called us back into the room and gently informed us that my father was close to the end. Nurses have a way of knowing by tracking subtle shifts in breathing and changes to the body. My mom and I stood at the foot of the bed while the nurse took my father's pulse with her fingertips. After a few minutes, I glanced toward the nurse and said, "He's gone. Isn't he?" Surprise washed over her face as she replied, "Actually, yes."

I sensed the moment my father's soul left his body. It wasn't a visual thing. It was *knowing*. His *body* was lying in that bed—all eighty pounds of him. But *my dad* was gone. After many years of leaning into my faith and believing in an afterlife or heaven, I started to understand and truly *believe* in the difference between the mind, the heart, the soul—and whatever lies beyond. And that's when I thought, *okay, something shifted here.*

At that moment, I knew and understood something beyond myself. That faith was now just shown to me in real life, there was no doubt. All that I had been taught as a kid in church, the soul, an afterlife, a future after we pass, became real to me. Knowing Dad was gone before the nurse told me was all the evidence I needed.

For me, that's when my faith took over. I didn't *see* anything; I didn't *think* anything; I just *sensed* something and knew it was true: there *is* a higher power with a plan for us.

Faith Gives Me Confidence

Having faith has *given* me faith. I trust that leaning into God and His plan will help me realize my boldest dreams. For example, at the beginning of 2022, faith encouraged me to act on one of my ambitions: to increase my charitable giving. This is one of the most admirable traits I picked up from my mom. I was already donating to four charities near and dear to my heart. Still, I'd been itching to increase my contributions. Journaling had stirred up a specific number. As I thought about it daily, that number would not go away. Was this God? I believe it was.

Calling upon my faith, I committed to donating that specific amount by the year's end. No one knew about this goal other than me and God. I was exhilarated and terrified. To hit my giving goal, every one of my prospective clients and commissions would have to come through that year. The fact is, I had no idea how I was going to pull this off, but I knew I had to try. I held on to my faith that this was the right move at the right time and that God had a plan for me. My faith paid off. Not only did my clients and commissions come through, but I *exceeded* my financial goals for 2022. When I set these goals, I did not believe it would be possible to exceed them. Yet here I was, leaning on my faith and achieving beyond my highest aspirations.

Because of such experiences, faith has given me the confidence to pursue remarkable things and make bigger, bolder strides. Through my faith, I genuinely believe I have a strong, stable foundation, even when the world feels upside down—and the world usually feels upside down. Whether it's the weather, politics, religion, the economy, or the pandemic, life is filled with uncertainty—and it always will be. The only consistent things in life are change and God.

What do you hang on to when your world gets shaken up? Faith. Nothing *except* faith will do in the face of such uncertainty. If I hadn't had faith that God has a plan for me, I would have given up by now. Even with faith, I still have troubled moments. But faith is a loyal companion during these times. There is no harm in believing that your higher power has a plan for you. It's time to delve into your faith and see where it leads.

Nurturing my faith has changed my life. Now I want it to change yours. I want you to dig deeper into *your* faith.

Call to Create Awesome: Faith

When you have faith, taking uncertain steps toward your goals, dreams, and desires is easier. Faith allows you to take positive steps in the direction you dream of without necessarily understanding where it will lead or why you're doing it.

I'd love you to use your journal to take stock of your faith. What matters to *you* about faith? What is your definition of faith, and how can you nurture it? It's not about what your parents say. It's not what your neighbours say. You have to take responsibility for your *own* beliefs. And that means you'll reach different conclusions than I did. You might have a different relationship with faith than I do, and that's fine. I want you to *have* an intentional, intimate relationship with faith and be able to call upon it in times of need.

Keep returning to this exercise to see how you grow and expand your faith. If you feel stuck, check out my example at the end of the chapter.

Take the first step: Find a place to get quiet and limit external distractions and noises. That means putting your phone away. Listen to your heart, yourself, and your higher power. When you're quiet, God will show you what you're supposed to be doing and the actions you're supposed to take. Be aware of what you, God, or the universe is trying to tell you.

Then, using the following journal prompts to think more deeply about faith.

- Consider the word *faith* and begin writing whatever comes to mind. Don't worry about spelling or grammar. Don't even worry about writing down complete thoughts. You can write short sentences, doodle pictures, or even create a mind map. You can share stories and anecdotes on faith, add quotes you like, or ask yourself questions. In a freestyle writing exercise, anything goes. There are no rules about what to write.

- How does it feel to call on something invisible, like faith?

- What helps me keep faith alive?

- Where do I find faith? How can I find faith when I need it most?

If it's still a challenge, don't worry; it takes practice. Commit to a continuous, repetitive time to journal. Start with a thirty-day commitment, then move forward. Please keep returning to this exercise to see how you might grow, expand, or notice more each month or week.

The good news is that next, we get to talk about something concrete: Goals.

SAMPLE JOURNAL RESPONSE

Where do I find faith? How can I find faith when I need it most?

One place I find faith during dark or challenging moments is in music. I love singing, especially harmonies. Quartet harmony makes the hair on my arm stand up. I feel more connected to my faith, confidence, and calmness whenever I sing, which becomes a reality. The world's issues disappear when I sing.

I feel the same way when I listen to music. Songs jump out at me, and I pay attention; it could be the melody, the chords, the harmonies, or the words. The lyrics often stick with me for a long time. I love to dig deep into the heart and soul of a song. I've been known to listen to the same song on repeat during a three-hour drive. I love to figure out if I'm being sent a piece as a message from above. Who else needs to hear this song? Why am I attracted to this song?

After my mother passed away, I had one song in particular that I listened to all the time. "Scars in Heaven by Casting Crowns. This song refers to the fact that my mom was no longer in pain, and the "scars" she gained through life were no longer causing her pain. That song provided solace and healing, and it kept me connected to my faith, and faith was one of the few things that got me through my grief. Even now, when I hear that song, it brings me close to mom.

2

Goals

"An aim or desired result."

At the beginning of 2022, I set *lofty* personal and business goals. Honestly, I even surprised myself. A lot of things needed to come together to meet them. And rarely, if ever, do so many things come together at once. But in 2022, they did.

2022 was the year we closed the biggest one-time deal of my life: the acquisition and merger of a successful insurance brokerage by Benson Kearley IFG. It was on the horizon at the beginning of the year, but many things had to come together to make it happen. I've been in this business for over forty-eight years and have had some great successes, but this merger deal was among the most satisfying. And it was also the most personal.

Before Benson Kearley, I worked at Bryson Insurance. I was there for almost eight years and felt exceptionally close to the owner and president, Tracy Makris, who brought me in as Vice President of Strategic Growth Initiatives. Working at Bryson and with Tracy, I gained confidence as a leader. It was a wonderful experience, and I valued going to work every day.

But after about six years, things shifted in the company culture. I'd grown a lot while at Bryson, worked with leadership I admired, and the office was filled with people I'd become close to, but the job at Bryson was no longer the right fit for me, and I struggled to accept that fact. It was a challenging time. Early one morning, I was at the office drinking my coffee and journaling. I looked around and asked myself, "Doug, can you see yourself here five years from now?" And in a split second, I knew the answer: *No, I can't.*

I knew I had to leave at that point, but I was still scared to leap. I was fifty-eight years old. I expected to be at Bryson my entire life. Even worse, I knew Tracy would be disappointed with my decision. Still, I knew it was time. After doing years of journaling—using these eight words and techniques—I knew I had to set one truly important goal: to leave Bryson as respectfully and professionally as possible.

After setting that goal, I decided what measures to implement to meet it. I went to the nearest coffee shop and sat for about three hours to write down my exit strategy, which I felt would be the most respectful to the team and my clients and beneficial to the company. Then, I laid out the plan for Tracy. She accepted it even though she was disappointed. As a result, my transition out of Bryson went smoothly. My respect for Tracy grew, and we dealt with the change professionally. It was an emotional time for me, as I had become close to the entire Bryson team.

The first year after I left Bryson, Tracy and I rarely spoke. We only communicated when we had to discuss business or clients. Despite a clean break, it felt like another divorce. I was disappointed, but I knew I'd left with great intention and integrity and had shown great care for Tracy. However, I still worried that the way I went fell short of my goal. Fortunately, it turns out that if you make hard choices with intention, time will heal all wounds. After a while, Tracy and I started sending emails just to check-in. Then we'd reconnect over lunch here and there. Eventually, we were back to normal—a new normal—but the personal and professional bond that Tracy and I shared was still there, and I was grateful for that.

We stayed in touch like this for a few years, and then one day in 2021, Tracy called me and wanted to get together for lunch. I didn't think much of it because we had enjoyed other lunches by then. We had a lovely meal, and then Tracy's voice changed. I knew she was about to get serious, so I put my drink down. Tracy wanted to know if Steve and I would like to buy Bryson at Benson Kearley. Tracy greatly admired Steve Kearley due to our previous dealings and felt confident in who he was—and who I am. I was floored. Even though it had been five years, I still knew most of the people at Bryson and had great relationships with them. I'd be working with my old friends and colleagues again. It was a dream come true and something I never thought possible.

Making the deal was a once-in-a-lifetime experience. I kept thinking, *Wow, Doug, when you left, you did it right.* This acquisition would never have happened if I hadn't treated Tracy respectfully during my exit. Tracy told me, "I'm ready to sell, but I'm not going to sell to anybody." Bryson was the brokerage her father built, and Tracy so capably managed, so the buyer mattered. Tracy doubled down on her position as we talked: "I'm only going to sell if it's to you. Period." So, in July 2022, we closed the deal to buy Tracy's brokerage. It's the largest acquisition Benson Kearley has ever made. By setting one simple goal—to leave Bryson in a considerate and respectful manner—I created an enormous opportunity for Benson Kearley IFG and me. I call situations like this a strategic by-product of doing what is right. Good things multiply into additional good things.

I've always been a goal-setter. Part of that comes from my business background: I started in sales, which is a goals-driven role. Through my professional success, I've grown to believe that if you want to positively impact your life and work, you must have *something* to shoot for.

Become the Person Who Achieves Their Goals

Goal setting also comes from my desire to be better today than I was yesterday. I had no idea that, five years after leaving Bryson, Tracy would invite us to buy the entire firm. I didn't plan a kind and professional exit because I expected to be rewarded for it—I did it because it has always been my goal to treat people as they deserve to be treated.

Here's a fact that may surprise you: it's not the goal that matters. What counts is the growth and change you experience when striving for that goal. Jim Rohn, who was an inspirational leader in the United States, said, "The ultimate reason for setting a goal is to entice you to become the person it takes to achieve it."

This chapter will teach you the importance of setting goals. If you set goals and have faith that you'll achieve them, you will surpass them. Even more important, you will become the person who achieves them.

As a salesperson, I always set a goal to make a certain amount in sales each year, which is standard for my profession. Sometimes, I had to change my process or methods to meet my goal. Perhaps I had to focus on new insurance coverage or a different industry. Likewise, I needed to evolve and change to become a better *person*. I had to become the kind of person who met my goals. I needed to be not just a goal-setter but a goal-achiever.

The same applies if you want to lose weight: you have to become the kind of person who can lose weight. It would be best if you changed your habits: commit to exercise and watch what you eat. Taking the initial steps can be a challenge. It's often a slow process. But if you keep taking those steps, you'll notice a transformation happening over time, not only in your body but also in your character: you started with a goal to lose weight and become someone with discipline.

A Tried-and-True Method for Goal Setting

In 2000, I joined a coaching company called Strategic Coach to help me with my overall business growth and planning. Dan Sullivan and Babs Smith founded it. Over the years, Strategic Coach has developed tools to help entrepreneurs think and plan. One of the Strategic Coach tools I still use today is the Annual Planner, which involves setting and reviewing your goals every ninety days. Every quarter, I evaluate my old goals and make new ones. Being intentional and consistent like this is a large part of my success. I love this worksheet, but I recognize that unique styles and techniques motivate people, so feel free to find or create your methodology for setting goals.

When I set goals, I write them down by hand. Writing longhand is the single most important thing I do because it slows me down. I've made some of my most important discoveries when slowing down and tapping into a calm, quiet mind. Science tells us that writing by hand also builds sixteen times more neural pathways in the brain, which means I'm more likely to remember and achieve what I've written. I've had goals happen that I've forgotten about, yet somehow, they came to fruition. I like to think that when I take the time to be intentional and write my goals down longhand, I am consciously and subconsciously moving toward those goals.

Whatever your methods, you must have measurable goals to orchestrate an intentional life that keeps moving you forward. The Strategic Coach's Annual Planner suggests setting ten yearly goals. There is room to answer the question, *WHY? Why does this goal matter?* If I don't know *why* I'm setting a goal, it's not important enough. My goals need purpose because that's when my heart takes over and helps me act on the habits, changes, and approaches that will help me meet my goal.

The next set of columns on the sheet is divided into quarters. Since Strategic Coach recommends working in ninety-day cycles, I must ask myself, "What will I do in the next three months to push my goal forward?" Reviewing this form at least every ninety days will help me stay focused and be intentional about my actions.

Every ninety days, I analyze if I was successful in moving towards the goal. Did I do what I needed to do to complete my goal? I don't beat myself up if I didn't reach my goal the previous quarter. Instead, I challenged myself by asking what I needed to modify to reach my goal this quarter. *How do I recalibrate or break down my goals to become more achievable in the next ninety days?*

I have two goal sheets: one is for my business goals, and the other is for my personal goals. I look at them regularly and focus on more detail every ninety days. If you make this your practice, you *will* meet most of your goals. The reason? You're focused, you're setting goals that matter, and you're intentional about pursuing them.

B-HAGs: Big, Hairy, Audacious Goals

Many people are afraid of setting goals because they are afraid of failing to achieve them. Deep down inside, they wonder, *What happens if I set a goal and fail to meet it?* To answer that, let's return to Jim Rohn's quote: "The ultimate reason for setting a goal is to entice you to become the person it takes to achieve it."

Let me be clear: even if I don't make a goal, I've had some growth, and I've gained something of value. John Maxwell says, "Sometimes you win, sometimes you learn." With many years of personal and professional successes, I can assure you it's not,

"Sometimes you win, sometimes you lose." Life is not a zero-sum game. I might not achieve ten goals in ninety days or even in a year if I set ten goals, but I move the needle towards the success of that goal, and I am making progress. But if I take even one step toward that goal—if I change my habits, develop more discipline, or start to learn a new skill—*that's a win.* It might not be the win I had in mind, but it *is* a win. (Strategic by-products) Sometimes, by completing a task or a goal, you will achieve something that was not intended but is still a great addition or win due to your win. This book is a strategic by-product of many things in my life. I never intended to write or become an author, but as a result of my journaling, I am here.

Sometimes, for this reason, I think it's fun to set one or two goals so wild, imaginative, and unrealistic that I can't achieve them in my normal thinking mind. I like to call these B-HAGs—big, hairy, and audacious goals. I haven't achieved my B-HAGs in many years, but I have reached for more by setting them. In 2022, I did have some big, hairy wins, but they weren't because of the planning and goal setting I did that year. It was because of the planning I had been doing for the last *ten* years. The effect of setting my goals compounds over time. It's the gift that keeps on giving. Have I made all my goals every year? Of course not. But sometimes, setting the wheels in motion takes a few years.

What If I Fail?

In 2021, my top goal was to get in better physical shape. I could stand to lose a few pounds, and now that I'm over sixty, I feel it's vital to stay on top of my health. I planned to hire a personal trainer, but the year got away, partially due to the pandemic, and I didn't meet my goal. So, guess what was at the top of my goals for 2022? The same thing: take care of my health and lose weight. Instead of beating myself up for failing to meet my goal, I got even *more* motivated. I used my failure as fuel and attacked my goal with gusto. I hired a trainer and hit the gym every Monday and Wednesday, and I lost twenty pounds before the fourth quarter.

Who cares if I didn't make my goal in 2021? The goal was important to me; I had my "why," so I just kept at it in 2022. Now that 2022 is over, I can look back and say, "Doug, it took you a little longer than originally planned, but you did it. You lost twenty pounds. You're one hundred times stronger than you were last year. You feel better and more confident." Those are what I like to call the "strategic by-products" of setting your goals. Even if I lost ten pounds or five, making an effort was worth it.

So, set B-HAGs, small, achievable goals, and everything in between. The point is that if you select and pursue your most meaningful goals, you will be much further along in creating an awesome life than someone who doesn't. Over time, you will enjoy the fruits of that compounding effect when you meet and exceed bigger and wilder goals than you ever thought possible.

So, what if you fail to meet a B-HAG or any of your goals? Remember that five out of ten is better than zero; in other words, at least you're making progress. Failure is part of the growth process. If you aren't failing, you aren't growing.

Getting Quiet Pays Off

If you had told me five years ago, "Doug, you're going to write a book. You're going to have an idea you care about, be attached to people that will help you see it through, and you're going to have the finances to pursue it." I would have laughed at you.

A few people have told me I should author a book through the years, but the timing or subject matter never felt right. The person who advocated for that most was my mother, Pat. She wanted me to share my "create awesome" strategies. I wasn't sure I had enough to say, and I didn't feel ready, so I put that goal aside for years. But the idea was still ruminating in my head and heart. Then, in October 2021, my mom passed away, and not long after her funeral services, I was sitting in Starbucks journaling. While quietly reflecting on my mother's life, it hit me—it was time to write a book.

I sucked it up, took out my Strategic Coach worksheets, and set a goal to write *Create Awesome*.

Still, I had nagging doubts. I thought, *Doug, you're talking about a book here. That's a big undertaking.* I shook it off and hit right back at that anxious thought: *Don't worry about the work yet; just set the goal. Then, take the next step.*

I got home that night to find a good-sized envelope in the mailbox. Inside was a complimentary copy of the book Dan Sullivan from Strategic Coach had recently published. When I read the title in big, bold letters, the hair on my arms stood up: *Big Book Payoffs: Why Every Entrepreneur Should Write a Book.* The words *holy crap* flew out of my mouth. Right then and there, I told the universe, "Alright, I see what you're trying to do here, and I'm listening." First, I set a mental goal to author this book. Then I took out my journal and wrote it down in ink.

Moments like this are when you have to stay focused and aware. These are the clear-as-a-bell signs you get from the universe, God, or whatever higher power you have faith in when it's time to set a new goal and embark on a new adventure. So, I did. And here I am today, taking it step by step to reach that goal. Because when the universe tells you it's time to do something, you've got to see it through.

Call to Create Awesome: Goals

It took me years to reach the point of regularly exceeding my goals. With the wins in 2022, when Benson Kearley IFG bought out Bryson, I finally did—and that's part of the inspiration for authoring this book. In eventually exceeding my goals regularly, all the arduous work I put into creating awesome things using these eight tenets is finally showing some continual results.

Most people have an underlying sense that they can improve their lives. The only problem is they don't know what they *want* out of life. For so many, it can be hard to separate dreams and desires from social or familial pressure or what they've seen others achieve. That's why it's good to take the time to ask yourself: *What do I want to improve about my life right now, and what can I do to achieve that?*

It's critical to set mindful, personal goals to answer that question. You can't understand how to improve the quality of your life without explicitly outlining the goals and outcomes that will bring about that improvement.

Meeting and exceeding goals is a *process*. It takes time, so *now* is the best time to start. Setting goals today means the positive results will compound next week, month, and year. And trust me when I say you won't even be able to imagine where you end up a *decade* from now.

Take a few minutes each day to reflect on your goals for the next thirty days. When you set aside intentional time to write and review your goals, they become clearer and more achievable. Just as with faith, putting something into practice and seeing it happen builds confidence, which I'll discuss more in chapter seven.

So, ask yourself: *What are my goals? What matters to me right now?* Remember, you need to do this exercise regularly. Your goals won't be the same now as they were five years ago, and they won't be the same five years from now. Your ambitions, dreams, and desires change and grow as you do. Growth changes everything.

The only way I've ever figured out what matters to me is to sit down and ask myself real questions—and be honest with the answers. If you do the same, you'll be surprised by what comes up.

Take the first step: Use your journal to note goals you have now or new ones you've been afraid to think about, let alone write down. Find a place to get quiet and limit external distractions and noises. (Reminder: put your phone away!) Listen to your heart, yourself, and your higher power. When we're quiet, God will show us what we're supposed to do and the actions we're supposed to take. Be aware of what you, God, or the universe is trying to tell you.

Then, use the following journal prompts about goals.

- Do a freestyle writing exercise on the word *goals*.

- Pick your top ten goals, personal or business.

- Answer the question *Why?* For each goal. If you can't answer that question, pick another goal. This will help you set intentions and clarify what's important to you.

- Then, write down your personal and professional goals for the next ninety days. Be sure to mark your calendar so you circle back to them in three months.

You can do this exercise by hand at the end of each chapter or use the extra blank journal pages in this book. I suggest revisiting your goals quarterly.

This allows you to modify and update your goals as you move forward.

It's time to clarify what you want from life and confidently walk in that direction. But don't forget about others along the way. We'll discuss that in the next chapter.

> **SAMPLE JOURNAL RESPONSE**
>
> 1. I need to feel better physically. If I feel better, I will feel more confident.
>
> 2. I need to educate myself on a certain topic. This will allow for more business opportunities.
>
> 3. I need to build my network to open more doors.
>
> What are the *Whys?* Attached to these? If you accomplish these three goals, how does this improve your life and make you feel better?

3

Giving

"To present voluntarily and without expecting compensation."

When I was a teenager, Jim Crawford and his wife, Isabel, were the counsellors of a youth group at our church. Participating in that youth group was a transformative experience, particularly because of Jim and Isabel's leadership. Their presence came at just the right time and place in my life. Like most kids, I was an uncertain teenager looking for acceptance and guidance, and I found it in the community that Jim and Isabel created.

The group consisted of about a hundred kids aged twelve to twenty, and Jim and Isabel opened their home to *all* of us. If we had an issue, we went to them. They were the easiest grown-ups to talk to and always had time and energy to give. Jim was an electrician who owned a company that was doing well financially and shared liberally with others. And yet, despite how much of their time, money, and resources the Crawfords gave, their lives always seemed full. To this day, our youth group still stays connected through regular emails. Unfortunately, those messages often involve sharing that one of our parents has passed or some other difficult news, like a concerning medical diagnosis. But the desire to stay connected shows what an indescribable bond we share.

One ordinary Wednesday evening during a youth group meeting, Mr. C (as we called him back then) said something that stuck with me and everyone in that room: "Kids, you can never outgive God. He spoke with such gentle modesty and conviction. These were not just words spoken but lived and proved daily. Regardless of how much the Crawfords gave, they were always blessed beyond measure. Right then and there, I knew I would live my life by that guiding principle.

In my sixty-some-odd years, I have tested Mr. C's theory a few times and found it true. My goals from 2022, for instance, are a clear example of my deciding on a goal that, in my small mind, I had no idea how they would be possible. However, I felt the target was correct and had to accept that I wanted to make it happen. Jim Crawford's words inspired me to give more than I ever believed I could. Again, what's even more powerful is realizing that Mr. C didn't just *say* those words; he *lived* them. He gave freely, knowing he could never outgive God. Mr. C would never be without. Decades later, Mr. C's boundless generosity still profoundly influences me, and I strive to walk in his footsteps.

I've realized, over time, that the two concepts of faith and giving are connected in an eternal cycle. These are two of the most important words I journal about daily. I want to know who needs help and where resources are needed. I have learned that if I draw on my faith and put the work in, I will always have enough time, money, and resources to give. My faith calls on me to pull in love and resources to help replenish, fortify myself, and fill my reservoir. As the reservoir is being loaded, it is important to look for directions for how it will be used. It's time to share once you've received these things and built yourself up. While faith is the pulling in, giving is the pushing out so that you can begin the cycle anew. You can empty your reservoir by helping others because you have faith that your pool will fill again. I don't ever worry about my reservoir. I trust and believe God will fill it as needed to do what he asks of me. He won't ever ask without providing the means. Everything I have is from God. I am the caretaker of the resources; these resources do not belong to me; I am their manager. I need to get quiet and listen to know how and where God wants the resources used. That is an enormous responsibility, one I do not take lightly.

In this chapter, you'll learn how to set a giving mindset and how it can improve your life.

DOUGLAS W. BUNDOCK

Set a Giving Mindset

People give for varied reasons. Some want acknowledgement; they want to be on the newspaper's front page, handing off an oversized cheque. Is giving sometimes about helping, or is it about satisfying their ego? While I try not to judge, in the end, I believe that silent giving is how we should give. It is not really about us anyway.

My mom was a silent giver. She was an entrepreneur, the best salesperson in our family, and she loved to make money—but not for the sake of having it. Instead, she loved to use the money to bring joy to the people and community around her.

I took over managing my mom's finances after my dad passed away in 2000, and I couldn't believe what I found. The amount of money she donated to charitable organizations and loved ones in a year, without fanfare, was astounding. The *only* reason I knew was that I had to manage her accounts. During our few conversations about philanthropy, my mom clarified that her core value was caring for others using her resources. She never felt the money she earned was for her and hers alone. Instead, my mother believed that much of the abundance received belonged to a spiritual web, and Mom's desire was to pass it along in that great chain of giving. She always had faith that her reservoir would be full.

After my mom passed away in October 2021, more stories of her quiet generosity emerged. Though she never told a soul, she was known for paying for the groceries of someone standing in front of her in line at the checkout. In addition, my mom loved to buy nice clothes and give them away, a fact I didn't learn until her funeral. Oh, I knew she was a clotheshorse who loved to get dressed up. I once built a walk-in closet for her so she could keep her clothes clean and organized. But I didn't know that friends would stop by and go shopping in her closet. She sent them home with an armload of designer clothes—often with the tags still on. Hearing story after story about her generosity while I was grieving was a gift. Even in death, my mother's chain of giving kept going.

Thanks to my mom, giving is in my DNA, but she didn't inherit it from her parents. She didn't live a charmed life—quite the opposite. My grandfather was a heavy drinker, and my grandmother ran a strict Pentecostal home. Since her home life was challenging, my mom worked hard to create a more stable environment for my brother and me. As I mentioned earlier, my mom also endured the loss of her two-year-old daughter. That pain stayed with her for the rest of her life. My mother had every reason to withdraw her gifts and refuse to share with the world, but instead, she gave—and gave freely. My mom always knew she could create more. Being a giver was her way of creating awesome friends, loved ones, and even strangers. You see, "the better parts of her life live on through me," something I'll discuss more in the chapter on the legacy.

The Cost of Giving

Here's a little secret about giving: It doesn't cost much. You have more to gain by being generous. That might sound strange. After all, we offer something at no cost without asking for anything in return. And usually, that "thing" has value, monetary or otherwise. So, how can the benefit outweigh the cost?

Maybe you volunteer a few hours or donate a few hundred dollars—that may not be a lot compared to how much time and money you have. But the rewards of that generosity are staggering. Once you get into the habit of giving, you'll notice a pep in your step because you feel like you're contributing—and you *are* contributing. You'll glow because you believe you are making a difference—and you *are* making a difference. And you'll wake up feeling lighter because you realize that you matter—and you *do* matter. Developing an intentional habit of philanthropy and generosity will build confidence and create more meaning in your life.

When I feel good emotionally, physically, and mentally, and my inner reservoir is full, I prioritize giving. But giving works just as well, sometimes even better, when my reservoir and internal resources run low. When I'm feeling down or depleted, engaging in a simple act of giving flips my mentality immediately; it alters my whole being. That's because generosity forces me off the hamster wheel long enough to think about somebody or something else. We usually believe we have nothing to give when down and out. And yet, the moment I give, I realize the abundance at my disposal. By getting outside of myself and staying connected to the needs of others, I remain conscious of how much I have.

Keep It Simple and Consistent

Giving doesn't have to be an over-the-top act. It's often not. When I started asking myself about creating awesome, I quickly realized that one way to create awesome in *my* life is by creating it in the lives of others—you can successfully create awesome through simple, humble acts. I've found that even these small acts reverberate in unexpected ways. For example, I love giving people my favourite books (I'm known in some circles as "The Book Guy"). I give them away like sticks of chewing gum. No matter where I work, I ensure my office has a fully stocked shelf called the Giving Library. This library is where I immediately keep copies of my most cherished titles to give to friends, colleagues, and loved ones.

In their book *The Dash*, authors Linda Ellis and Mac Anderson ask, "When your life is over, everything you did will be represented by a single dash between two dates—what will that dash mean for the people you have known and loved?" I came across the book during a challenging time, and it helped me focus on what mattered most. While I was still at Bryson for Christmas one year, I bought a copy for the team of about thirty-five people. The holidays came and went in a flash like they always do, so I quickly forgot about this gift.

A few weeks after the winter break, our receptionist, Priya, stopped by my office to tell me she'd read *The Dash*. She thanked me and then held out her arm. She'd gotten a tattoo inspired by *The Dash*—the year she was born, written in Roman numerals, followed by the iconic dash. Priya told me, "This is my reminder to be careful of what my dash is and to make my dash matter."

I never expected this breezy gift-giving gesture to result in us standing in my office near tears! I couldn't believe it. Thirty-four other people got the book. Maybe it impacted them; perhaps it didn't. But that didn't matter to me because it affected *one* person.

That was the first time I asked myself, "How do I create more awesome things in my life and in others?" That experience taught me I could do amazing things with my life. Using the act of giving to create awesome in my community is one way I've kept that sense of awe and amazing things going.

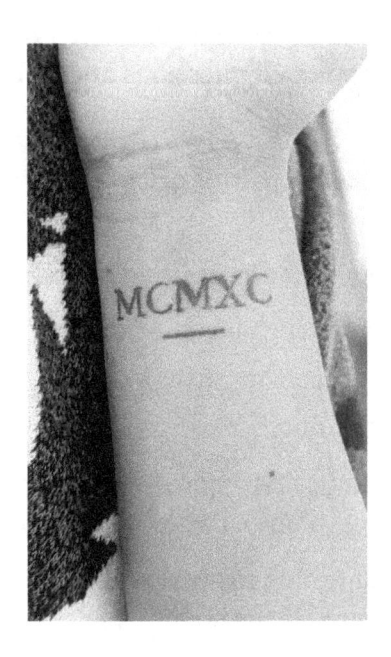

Call to Create Awesome: Giving

Set a goal to commit a few intentional acts of giving over the next ninety days.

Take the first step: Use your journal to note acts of giving or receiving you engage in. Find a place to get quiet and limit external distractions and noises. (Lose the phone, remember?) Listen to your heart, yourself, and your higher power. When we're quiet, God will show us what we're supposed to be doing and the actions we're supposed to take. Be aware of what you, God, or the universe is trying to tell you.

Let this calm, peaceful moment inspire your writing. Ask yourself questions and be honest with the answer:

- Do a freestyle writing exercise on the word *giving*.
- What does the word, *giving* mean to me?
- What types of giving do I find important?
- Who will I give to a friend, a stranger, or my community?
- What am I going to give? Will it be related to resources, money, or time?
- How am I going to give? Will I give in a way that is outside the box?
- What acts of giving do I already engage in?

Use your goals sheet to create at least one giving goal you want to reach for the next ninety days.

- During those three months, note how taking intentional steps towards generosity has felt.
- Check back in three months to see your progress on that goal.
- Ask yourself: *Has faith played a role in me achieving this giving goal?*

SAMPLE JOURNAL RESPONSE

A few years ago, I created my own Create Awesome journals. They are leather-bound, come in many colours, and have the emblem embossed on the front. I never attend a meeting without a journal or two and pay attention to who might need one. I never intended to sell them; I give them away. My goal was not to profit but to make a difference. To date, I have given more than 1,000 journals away.

If I can provide a means of helping someone start to write and think, then that is, in my mind, Creating Awesome.

Jeff Paterson (my best friend at the office and one of the kindest people you'd ever meet) and I sometimes put the coffee on for everyone first thing in the morning. It's a small thing we like to do for our colleagues. We'd grind the beans, put them in the filter, fill the water, and before long, we'd have a big pot of caffeine to share with the team. It warms everyone up and brings them a little joy. Some days, I don't feel like I have much to give, but I need to remember I always have enough to "put on a pot of coffee" for the people in my life.

We must be servants daily, not just when we feel like it.

4

Kindness

"Being selfless, caring, compassionate, and unconditionally kind."

In my line of work, I sometimes deal with upset clients. When they call with raised voices and a threatening tone, it's easy, even understandable, to react negatively to them.

But when someone is upset, it's most important to treat them with kindness. We have no idea what else is going on behind the scenes. I remember that their insurance issues are only a part of the client's emotional state, and multiple stressors are contributing to their anger. There are insurance brokers out there who find these calls a nuisance. But they miss out on connecting with their clients when it matters most.

When a client calls in angry, the first thing I do is show compassion and empathy. I will listen intently to their problem and refrain from saying a word. I use professionalism and humour to break the anger. Listening intently to them speak and allowing them to vent helps them know I care. From there, I can figure out where and how I can help. Their problem might be related to their insurance, or they might be unhappy with the result of a claim settlement. Usually, I can do at least one or two things to help my client, and we find those solutions much more quickly when I approach a tense situation with kindness and empathy.

Operating from a place of empathy calms the situation for *both* of us. It enables me to be kinder to my clients and myself. Staying calm is good for me too! I want to help—part of being a servant is to help—and unless I listen, I can't know how to help. Because they feel cared for in their moment of need, these clients often work with me for years and become some of my most loyal customers.

The world is not a kind place; sometimes, it's cruel. But if you adopt a mindset of kindness, you increase your bandwidth to sit through difficult moments. If anger and stress take over, it can hurt my well-being. Every day, I write about being kind. Kindness can be a mindset and a way of life. My initial response to everything is to be kind. Doing so gives me the strength to solve personal and professional challenges gracefully.

Being kind is about something other than doing a respectable job in your business. It would help if you led with kindness in every aspect of your life. When you keep kindness as a core value, you see challenges as an opportunity to serve. This chapter will outline strategies for inviting more kindness into your life.

Apply the Golden Rule to Everyone

We all experience hardships. We may struggle to get out of bed in the morning or feel sad. What brings us back from the edge of despair? It's often the kindness and compassion of others. It also works the other way: we may never know why someone is having a difficult day, but we do know how to treat them: how we want to be treated. That's the Golden Rule and following it may be the thing that relieves them.

The reverse is also true: if we don't follow the Golden Rule and are not careful with our words and actions, we can hurt people in ways we don't even realize. Every religion has a version of the Golden Rule. Every higher power wants us to treat our fellow man with respect. I believe respect is the biggest thing lacking in the world today. Social media is full of disrespectful attitudes and negative and hurtful comments.

The problem is that some people don't have a high opinion of themselves and think they *deserve* to be treated poorly. Perhaps because they've been brought up in a dysfunctional home environment or suffer from self-esteem issues, does this sound familiar? If so, remember this: the Golden Rule applies to everyone—especially ourselves. We all deserve to be treated well. We must extend kindness and compassion to everyone, including ourselves. I mentioned the reservoir in a prior chapter, and it comes into play again here—we must be kind to ourselves to ensure the kindness reservoir is being filled continually. To properly treat others how you want to be treated, you must treat yourself respectfully. Once you learn how to treat yourself with kindness, you can extend that kindness to others—even those with different opinions who struggle to practice kindness themselves.

Plan Intentional Acts of Kindness

Do you want to know one of the most interesting things about kindness? You can *plan* to be kind. It's not something genetic—either you're kind or you're not. No, it's something you work at a little more each day. Being intentional about your kindness will make it a habit, and as a habit, kindness will become a reflex or an automatic instinct.

I call my planned moments "Intentional Acts of Kindness." Every morning, while journaling, I think about being kind and brainstorming ways to show kindness. The more I plan and execute these acts, the more they integrate into my day-to-day behaviour. Scientific studies show it takes twenty-one days to create a habit, but it takes ninety days for that habit to make a difference in our lives. I have certainly found this to be true.

I'm a nice enough guy, but I have my moments where I get tired, stressed, and busy. As I age, my tolerance level seems to be diminishing as well. Because I have intentionally worked on being kind, it's now easier to snap out of those stressed-out moments and let kindness guide my interactions. Being kind and compassionate has become who I am; the rewards are tremendous. I don't snap or leap all over people in person or online. In some ways, creating this new habit puts pressure on me to continue to be someone others look to for a sense of kindness and calm. Over the years, it has become more natural, but it was not always that way.

How can you start planning Intentional Acts of Kindness? The daily habit of journaling is where this can begin. We'll talk more about this in the Call to Create Awesome section, but here are some ideas to get the juices flowing.

Bring Awareness to Your Day

It's human and natural to fret over our problems. But when we're too focused on our lives, we miss what's happening around us and opportunities to be kind. Awareness *helps us* see and plan kindness.

One strategy to stay present and engaged when feeling fried is asking myself questions. I walk into work daily and say, "Doug, look alive. What's going on in the office? Who is close to tears? Who needs a one-on-one conversation? Who needs to laugh?" By paying attention, I've become good at reading people. I can walk through the office and tell what kind of mood my team is in. Having a sales background and being taught to read the buyer certainly helped, as success in sales depends on being good at reading people. To be this way, I have to get out of my head. My personal and sometimes even professional problems take a back seat at the office when dealing with a client or employee.

Our company has "huddles", which occur in person or online every Monday, Wednesday, and Friday. I run the Friday Zoom call. My number one goal during these "huddles" is to connect with my staff and show them appreciation, which means I must be aware when leading that call. I must pay attention to multiple faces on a screen while talking. It isn't always easy, but I work hard to ask myself awareness-raising questions and look for the answers. I will ask how someone is doing or coping with a specific issue. Sometimes, I can tell what's going on with a staff member through their body language, tone of voice, or even hair! Sometimes, on Zoom, I notice that someone who usually has the camera on does not, so I pay attention. I might send them an email afterward to check up on them. Sometimes, I can tell something is off by the person's smile—maybe it's not as big, or the person isn't smiling. These are all telling signs.

When I pick up on someone I suspect might be having a hard time, I set a goal to reach out to them. I might send a kind email, show recognition for their hard work, or offer them coffee. It doesn't have to be a grand, sweeping gesture. The point is to show my staff that someone is paying attention and cares—that *I* know them and their needs. These small ways of reaching out show kindness and incorporate two other tenets we have already discussed: goals and giving.

I also pay attention to how I come across on the phone and in emails. I take the time to revise my messages to ensure they are warm and friendly. Most of my emails start with a sincere and simple, "Hope you are well!" That statement was especially important to ask during the pandemic. We felt a little more caring about how others coped during the pandemic. We were all simultaneously going through a tremendous challenge, and no one knew what we were doing.

Unfortunately, I am scattered as I work on this book, so staying aware is more of a challenge. After I had COVID, I never really felt the same. Long COVID is taking its toll on me, allowing brain fog and lack of ability to focus to dominate more days than I would like. During times like this, I look inward and have some awareness of my needs. If I believe that I am scattered, then likely others are as well, for whatever reason. By using rest, reflection, and faith to fill my reservoir, I have more to give and more kindness to share.

I share this because *it's okay* if your awareness has lapsed. Fill yourself up to pay attention to what's happening around you. And once you see what's happening in your environment, you'll become more attuned to the moods and feelings of those around you. You can find ways to use kindness to elevate their mood from there.

Call to Create Awesome: Kindness

It's time to use your journal to consider how to bring more kindness into *your* life and the lives of those around you. Kindness can be found in acts of generosity and giving. For example, when my mom paid for the groceries of someone in the checkout line or shared her clothes. Kindness means offering someone a shoulder to lean on, holding a door open from a stranger, or offering a cup of coffee to your coworker.

Here's a way to incorporate goal setting into your kindness: after you brainstorm possible Intentional Acts of Kindness, strive to commit three over the next ninety days.

Take the first step: Find a place to get quiet and limit external distractions and noises. (Remember, lose the phone.) Listen to your heart, yourself, and your higher power. When you're quiet, God will show you what you're supposed to be doing and the actions you're supposed to take. Be aware of what you, God, or the universe is trying to tell you.

Use the following journal prompts to reflect on kindness.

- Do a freestyle writing exercise on the word "kindness."
- What brings out kindness in me?
- What makes me feel unkind?
- What am I aware of today?
- What acts of kindness can I plan for?

> ### SAMPLE JOURNAL RESPONSE
>
> *What makes me feel unkind?*
>
> I notice myself getting agitated when I spend too much time scrolling online. Increasingly, social media feeds are littered with people trying to boost their image or tear others down. Even worse, internet threads are filled with anonymous commenters saying and doing things they would never say in person. And yet, we're addicted to our devices. A friend once said, "I scroll and scroll, looking for something, but I don't even know what I'm looking for. But if I don't scroll, I feel like I'll miss something." *Everyone seems to suffer from FOMO—the Fear of Missing Out. I prefer the acronym JOMO—The Joy of Missing Out. The fact is, you are not missing out on anything.*

Somedays, when I get online, the world appears worse than ever. Especially when authority figures we should look up to act unkind. It encourages others to do the same. These days, I can't help but notice how many big personalities in business, politics, and media are negative, name-calling bullies. It sets a bad example.

If I notice that I'm starting to scroll mindlessly through one negative story after another, I want to be better at shutting my phone off and giving myself a break. I want to set a *different* example. It comes down to taking control of my thoughts, which dictate how I behave and feel. So, when I'm scrolling through more

negative than positive content almost always makes my thoughts more negative than positive. Taking in too much negativity shifts my perspective, and what goes in is also what comes out. My temperament is shorter in these moments, and my outlook is more cynical.

I have to be careful what I watch and listen to. So, I have very few social media accounts and internet subscriptions, and I want to keep it that way. I've noticed that taking daily steps to limit my media diet has helped me be kinder and gentler to those around me.

5

Gratitude

"A strong feeling of appreciation."

In a world that often emphasizes the pursuit of material wealth and personal achievements, it is easy to overlook the simple act of gratitude. Cultivating a life full of gratitude can have profound and far-reaching benefits for our well-being. From enhancing our relationships and mental health to promoting resilience and personal growth, the practice of gratitude has the potential to transform our lives in remarkable ways.

We have all heard about a gratitude journal. While journaling daily, including the word gratitude and thoughts about gratitude, is important, I felt the need to journal about more than gratitude to have a larger impact on my life. That said, gratitude is a key topic and deserves its place in my top eight words.

What are the benefits of being grateful?

1. **Improved Mental Health:** Gratitude can be closely linked to improved mental and

emotional well-being. When we focus on the positive aspects of our lives and express gratitude for them, we shift our attention away from negativity. It has been proven that regularly practicing gratitude has been associated with reduced symptoms of depression and anxiety.

2. **Enhanced Physical Health:** Research shows that grateful individuals are more likely to engage in healthy behaviours such as regular exercise, proper nutrition, and sufficient sleep.

3. **Strengthened Relationships:** Gratitude fosters a sense of connection and appreciation, allowing us to build and maintain stronger bonds with family, friends, and colleagues. When we express gratitude towards others, it conveys our recognition and value of their presence in our lives, leading to deeper and more fulfilling relationships.

4. **Increase Resilience:** When we practice gratitude, we focus on what we have (our blessings) rather than what we lack. This mindset enables us to find meaning and perspective despite adversity, helping us bounce back from demanding situations.

5. **Personal Growth and Self-Esteem:** When we get intentional (my favourite word) about appreciating the blessings in our lives,

we become more aware of our strengths and abilities. Grateful individuals are more likely to set and achieve meaningful goals. We can take note of our positive journey and accomplishments.

Let me share a personal story involving my mom and some things that happened to help me put many things into perspective. It was May 26, 2018. I had a call from my mom's husband, Norman. (Mom married Norman about ten years after my dad passed away.) Norman had indicated to me that Mom had taken some new pain pills the night before, and he could not wake her up. Her breathing was shallow, and it was scary. I suggested that Norman call 911 and get some help. The help arrived quickly, and before long, my mom was in intensive care with very shallow breathing and a very faint pulse.

We met Norman at the hospital, and Mom was not doing well. Norman has a large Ziploc bag of medications with him. These were all the medications Mom was currently taking—thirteen in all. It seemed the night before, they had gone to a walk-in clinic to get some relief for some shoulder pain, and the new medicines added to what she was already on sent her to the edge of death. The doctors were not able to wake Mom up. They stopped all her regular medications and now had her intubated. Mom was, for all intense purposes, in an induced coma. She stayed like this for the next ten days. The doctors really could not understand why she was not waking up.

It was the next Friday evening, as I was sitting alone in the hospital room with Mom, I had this feeling Mom was gone. As I sat, I made notes on my phone of people I would need to call and things I needed to remember to do. Before I left late that night, I said goodbye to my mom. I just figured her life was over, and life as we have known for so long was about to change.

The very next day, Mom began to show signs of waking up. It was over the next three weeks that Mom gained enough strength to be transferred to a rehabilitation facility finally. She had come so close to death and had to learn how to be mobile again. On July 10, 2018, Mom went home. Miraculous; however, this is only part of the story.

During this entire time at work, I was in the process of losing some large accounts—client accounts that I had been fortunate to manage for many years. It was not anything I did personally to lose these, but insurance market conditions caused it. As much as this all was disappointing, my focus was on my mom.

I took a step back during that time and focused on what was important—not the business or the income it produced, but my mom. The lost clients can all be replaced, but my mom could not. In life, we fret about stuff that does not matter, even the things that can be replaced. I often wondered if losing those clients would have bothered me more if I had not been as focused on my mom then. It's sad to say that it probably would have. So, what did I learn from all of that? Be grateful daily for the things that matter—the things we take for granted, the amazingly awesome things that are not replaceable.

Another recent story hit me hard as I was authoring this book. The company I hired to help me go from a blank page to a published author began to lay off some of its staff. There seemed to be some reorganizing, but I was unsure what was happening. From what I started to see on LinkedIn, it appeared there was a chance the company might just shut down. I had already paid about 90 percent of the project fees and was still far from the finish line. Three very important people to me and the process, Anne, Sophie, and Meghan, seemed to me to be in a very vulnerable state.

My mind shifted from what seemed to be my problem to being concerned about my three partners. Their life had the potential for greater change than mine, for sure. I began to ask how they were coping and if they knew anything about their future. Even though I was in a precarious position, I was grateful because this was a passion project, not my full-time career. I could make that happen if I had to change gears to accomplish my end goal.

We must not lose focus on what matters again; things that can easily be replaced don't matter. People matter.

Sidebar:

It has occurred to me that a side hustle or passion project like this book should be taken more seriously than a part-time gig for many. If a person finds the time, their own time, to do something while not even being paid to do it, it matters a lot. Passion drives us. Perhaps this side hustle should not be a side hustle. It should be a more serious part of our lives. What if we could make enough money to live while working in our passion?

Going through this process, I reminded myself of the very real feelings that this book had to be written. That was still very real, and I will not be deterred. My passion for completing this book is real, and it will happen. I am unsure who or how it will be pushed over the finish line, but it will happen regardless.

Because I wear so many hats in the office, I must stay organized and be able to accomplish a lot on any given day. Years ago, I started creating a to-do list every day. This list helps me prioritize things and also helps me not forget things. I'm not getting any younger, right?!

A few years ago, I decided to rename my to-do list. I now call it my "get-to" list. These are not tasks that are a pain or cause me grief. I now look at the items on my list as things I am grateful to have the opportunity to complete. Whether the items are for a client or a team member, I am thankful for a large list. As I work through my list, I highlight the things completed. Highlighting completed items gives me a sense of satisfaction and accomplishment, and my brain says, "Well done." I am grateful to have influence and to make an impact daily.

I came up with the idea to rename my list while journaling one day. It all comes back to that quiet, reflective time. Ideas flow, creativity abounds, and different objectives are developed.

Call to Create Awesome: Gratitude

As you may have gathered, I have a serious coffee habit. Every morning, I hit the nearest coffee shop and spend a few minutes journaling about what I'm grateful for. I always start my journaling with gratitude. I am grateful for another day, health, strength, and breath. There are so many things we take for granted.

Creating this habit has trained my brain to seek out gratitude, which has created more positive awareness. It has helped me realize that there's always *something* to be thankful for, regardless of my situation. Gratitude, like faith, has helped me through some of the most difficult chapters of my life.

As mentioned earlier, the human brain has upwards of 60,000 thoughts daily, 80 percent of which are negative. Those same negative thoughts occur every day—imagine their compounding effect. Our thoughts are everything. It's time to take charge of them; we must change them daily. We're happier and healthier and contribute more to society when we're in a positive frame of mind.

One of the quickest ways to flip our thoughts from negative to positive is to practice gratitude. It's impossible to be grateful and negative simultaneously—those two don't play nicely together. So, dare to be grateful for the things in your life, great and small. Become aware of those little daily things you take for granted. You'll be amazed at what happens when you start journaling about your blessings.

Take the first step: Find a place to get quiet and limit external distractions and noises. (The phone is put away, right?) Listen to your heart, yourself, and your higher power. When you're quiet, God will show you what you're supposed to be doing and the actions you're supposed to take. Be aware of what you, God, or the universe is trying to tell you.

Then, use the following prompts to think more deeply about gratitude.

- Do a freestyle writing exercise on the word *gratitude*.

- What are the top five things I'm grateful for?

- What can I do to show gratitude towards somebody else?

Write down something you are grateful for every day for the next thirty days.

- Make a "Get-To" list: It's a simple shift, but recognizing that even my daily tasks are wonderful, challenging, and inspiring is an act of gratitude. I *get to* look after my clients today, have coffee with my colleagues, and spend time at work challenging my mind.

> **SAMPLE JOURNAL RESPONSE**
>
> We must be grateful for even the simplest things we take for granted.
>
> Family, food, a roof over our heads, our job, our colleagues, our country, our church, our friends, heat, hydro—the list can go on—and many of these things we take for granted.

6

Passion

"Intense emotion compelling action."

So many people think that passion is something they have or don't have. That could not be further from the truth. To discover your passion, you must seek it.

About fifteen years ago, my career interests changed, and I took a few messy and imperfect steps while hunting for my passion. I've been in the insurance business since I was eighteen, primarily in sales, but I also dabbled in management early on. In 2007, I worked at a brokerage that had recently been bought out, and I didn't fit in the new culture, so I went looking for an opportunity more aligned with my values.

So, I took a risk, went out to my network, and secured an interview at Willis Canada. I was thrilled. It was a new challenge and a managerial position with the opportunity for promotion. But when I was driving home from my second interview, I felt a tug in my spirit. Deep down, I knew going to Willis was the wrong move. It was outside my passion. But I ignored that gut feeling. I didn't know quite what my love was then, and I didn't want to listen to what my spirit had to say because I needed to leave my current brokerage. Plus, at the time, Willis was the third-largest insurance brokerage in the world. It was a prestigious place to land. So, when the offer finally came in, I packed up at my old brokerage, walked away from my clients, and took a leadership role at Willis.

To this day, leaving the clients I'd grown with and nurtured for twenty-five-plus years was, professionally speaking, the hardest thing I've ever done. I didn't fully appreciate how it would impact me. The minute I left, my former clients contacted me, looking for information about where I'd gone. It was bittersweet. I thought I was ready to move on, but instead, I felt like I had left my clients high and dry.

Still, based on the advice of others, I decided to wear the management hat exclusively and pursue that passion, so that's what I did. But a month into my new role, I realized the feeling while driving home after my interview was right. I had made a huge mistake. I missed my clients, and even though I had a passion for leadership, there needed to be a better fit than a senior management position at a large corporate firm.

At first, I lamented this mistake. On the inside, I beat myself up and told myself that I'd screwed up my twenty-five-year career. But on the outside, my life looked grand. The accolades for my new role kept coming in, and friends and colleagues patted me on the back. But I was miserable.

Finally, I sat down with my journal, got quiet, and asked myself, "What's important to me?" I realized I wanted to be a positively influential management person, but I also enjoyed chasing new sales. The real problem was that this was a large corporate position, an international brokerage with regulations to follow and multiple layers of executives pulling the strings. I started the insurance business in our small family brokerage, and Willis was miles from that. After some reflection, I knew I hadn't found my place or passion, so I had to stay on the hunt.

I journaled, conversed with trusted colleagues and advisers, and formed a new game plan. I knew I wanted to return to sales, but I decided the most respectful and responsible thing would be to stay at Willis for a year before leaving. So, one year later, I went to another brokerage, and over the next two years, I regained all my clients. I felt so encouraged by their response to me being back. At that moment, I knew that much of my passion revolved around serving people. In returning to sales, I had returned to myself. That servant mentality was part of my DNA, ingrained in me.

The funny thing was that after I left Willis, I got bored with only wearing one hat. I loved sales, but it wasn't enough. I missed the challenges of management. That's when I knew I had to find a job that gave me the best of both worlds—that perfect multi-hat role. Finding and living my passion took a while, but that's not surprising; I believe desires grow and change as we grow and change. I might not have known what made me tick if I had not made the "mistake" of going to Willis.

Remember when I said if you write goals down, the conscious and subconscious take over? The pursuit of my passion involved missteps and errors. And when I made those mistakes, I learned much more about Doug. So, what *was* my passion? Well, I discovered it was to impact my clients and team. Not just as an insurance broker but as a friend, a colleague, and a trusted adviser. That's how I ended up where I am today, deeply satisfied with my career and pursuing my passion simultaneously. I made it here because I went looking for my love and allowed myself to stumble and fall along the way. The mistakes also did not stop me. I *could* have recoiled and stayed stuck. But I chose not to do that, and my journaling practice helped. As we grow, our passions can change. Each part of life is a steppingstone. As we grow and learn, things change.

When I started in insurance, everyone told me I had to pick a lane—sales or leadership. They insisted I couldn't do both. Working at Willis, I realized that choosing a lane—not wearing two hats—was a mistake. I like wearing two hats. It keeps me from getting bored and is the secret of my passion. I want to do both.

Sales and management also satisfy another passion of mine: positively impacting the people around me, whether it's my clients or my direct reports. I'm an insurance broker because my dad was an insurance broker, and he helped me ply my trade. But is insurance my passion? Not really. I could be a lawyer, an accountant, or anything—it wouldn't matter so long as I could focus on my *passion* for serving. For me, the servant mentality has to be at the forefront.

I hunted for my passion, found it, and applied it to my job. So now, being an insurance broker and senior executive is a joy for me because I recognize both as the opportunity to serve others. And in my current role at Benson Kearley, I serve 100 people. These days, I feel like I'm at the *height* of my passion.

So, how do you find your passion? This chapter will take you through several techniques that put your search for your passion at the forefront of your life.

Start Your Hunt

Finding your passion is a complex line. You will make mistakes on your way to figuring out what drives you. But don't let that deter you. Like everyone else, you *need* to make mistakes to figure yourself out. If you're not making enough mistakes or even outright failing sometimes, you're not living life. Life is messy and imperfect, and so is finding your passion.

Moreover, your passions and interests change, and you must be willing to change and grow with them. That can be a messy process, too. I'm here to let you know it's okay to step out of line, make a mistake, and fix it as you search for the right place. When you think that you've ruined everything—you probably haven't. The only way to mess up finding your passion is by *not* starting. So, let's go! Here are two simple steps to get you on your way.

Ask Yourself the Big Questions

As I mentioned, I'm an insurance broker because my dad was an insurance broker, and I've had an amazing forty-seven-year career in this business, but it's because I've made this work *my own*. Like everyone else, I inherited certain beliefs and values. My life has been filled with specific events that molded me into who I am today. Even going through my divorce, I had choices to make. I figured out who I was. I had to identify my true self, separate from what my mother and father taught me to be. Different from what other people thought of me or wanted me to do. So, I asked myself some big questions: *What are my goals, and why do I care about them? How can I be kinder every day? What is my passion, and how can I pursue it? Where do I feel the most energy? Where am I contributing the most?*

As I considered these questions, I also thought when I was sure I had no future and had made too many wrong choices and mistakes. But I still didn't let those fears stand in my way. I still sought answers to my passion. Fear keeps us stuck in that rut. We refuse to leave lousy jobs or crappy relationships because of fear. But there is no rut if we're on the hunt for passion.

There are many stories about people who get burnt out on their high-profile corporate jobs and start a side hustle. *A side hustle* is a common phrase these days. As I commented in the previous chapter, side hustles are where a certain passion exists and who you want to be deep down inside. So, if your side hustle makes you happy, maybe it shouldn't be a side hustle—perhaps it should be your *main* hustle.

Ask Your Colleagues the Big Questions

One mistake people make is trying to figure their passion out alone. We can make the process much easier by enlisting our support system. Sometimes, our friends, family members, and colleagues can see things about us that we can't see in ourselves. Often, we don't know who we are; we see who we want to be or think we should be. Talking to others to find out what activities we're doing when we light up is important. Questions you might ask a colleague include: *What am I doing when I'm at my best? Is there a time when my energy level is effortlessly high?* Sometimes, when we're in the zone, we're oblivious to it. Asking our friends and colleagues to point out when we're in the zone can help us see it for ourselves.

People tell me I have the most energy and ease in front of the team. It could be connecting with one employee or the entire hundred-person team; my greatest energy source is the people around me. Over the years, recognizing this has helped me hone in on my pursuits. It has helped me focus on things I care about and get excited by, like public speaking and speaking off-the-cuff in front of groups.

People have also observed my passion when I talk about journaling. My friends, family, and colleagues say they see a difference in me when I talk about my practice. My eyes sparkle, my voice changes, and my spirit lifts. I hadn't noticed this on my own. A few weeks ago, one of my colleagues asked about this book. My expression instantly brightened as I told her about my new chapter. After a few minutes, she said, "Doug, you're on fire." I was on fire. My passion for the work came through as a clear and radiant spark.

A colleague recently came into my office just as I sat down to make notes for the book. He said, "Enjoy your writing time. I know it will make your day." And it did. It changed my entire day for the better. Authoring a book about journaling has ignited *my* passion for helping others discover *their* love. You see, it's not about journaling; it's about what journaling does to my heart, mind, and soul. It helps me define my life and what I want out of life. It makes me sit and think about things that are hard to deal with. I am still determining what happens after the book is written, but I know this is a steppingstone to something else. It could be a side hustle that will eventually become my main or semi-retirement hustle. But what matters is that I found a new outlet to help people.

So, take some time to ask your inner circle where they think your strengths and passions lie. Ask your friends, colleagues, and loved ones: *When am I on fire?* We'll talk more about this exercise in the Call to Create Awesome.

For now, we're on to one final truth about passion: you have to work hard for it.

Work Hard for Your Passion

Like everything in this book, living out your passion takes hard work, focus, and dedication. Just as you can become the person who meets a goal, you can become the person who lives up to their passion. Discover your passion, and then develop it.

Walt Disney approached over three hundred banks in pursuit of his dream: opening Disney World. He was rejected at every single one. The bankers thought he was mad. But Disney's wife pushed him to keep going, to visit more banks, and to leave no stone unturned. In other words, she urged him to do what was required to live out his passion. Pounding the pavement was demanding work, and the rejection was painful, but Walt Disney kept going at his wife's behest. Finally, bank number 304 gave Disney the financing; the rest is history. Would Disney have continued if he didn't have a passion? Of course not. That's how you work for your passion. That's how you create awesomely.

So, after you find your passion, put in the work to develop it; initially, my career was in insurance sales and service. I watched and listened to how other people did their job. I read books. I took courses to become better at both. As I moved into leadership roles, I had to learn new skills, so I took classes and attended seminars. I invested in building my skillset and talent, which is now paying off. Any work you put into your passion will pay off in dividends because *passion gives you energy*. It creates flow, ease, and, of course, awesome. As Simon Sinek says, "Working hard for something we don't care about is called stress. Working hard for something we love is called passion."

Think about a professional hockey player who has practiced every day since age five. (And yes, as a proud Canadian, I'm obligated to use hockey as a metaphor at least once in my book.) That player has spent hours honing his craft and has taken a lot of beatings, so he needs something to get him through the challenges, discomfort, and fatigue. He has the ultimate goal of making it to the National Hockey League. At any given time, there are about 700 players in the NHL. The odds of actually making it are slim. What separates those that make it from those that don't is one word: passion. The fire burning inside keeps them going even when it's physically and mentally grueling. You need enormous skill, but you get that by preparing, practicing, and working for it. The hockey player might come to practice exhausted but springs to life when he laces up his skates. By the time he hits the ice, practice doesn't feel like work anymore. It's a passion.

You can create this feeling in your own life because when you work hard to build on your passion, your passion will work hard for you. As you exercise your gifts, you will gain energy and confidence. Doors will open as others see your skill and unique flair.

Call to Create Awesome: Passion

I have read that 80 percent of people hate their jobs; they're only in their current jobs because they believe they must be. Many people start with something, and even if they're unhappy, they stick with it because it's easier to stay than pursue their passion. As mentioned earlier, passion takes work.

I talked about knowing I had to leave Bryson a few chapters back. It scared me to death to think about going. I was fifty-eight years old. I didn't have time to fix another huge mistake. I didn't know if I had the energy to start someplace new. I could have stayed. It would have been easier. Instead, I jumped in with both feet and never looked back. The work was worth it, and pursuing my passion made it easier. It gave me the energy to try something new.

We must remember we have a choice in how our lives unfold. We can find passion instead of waiting around for it to find us. Everyone needs a reason to get out of bed in the morning—to want to *get up*. Sure, we physically leave our bed, but do we bounce up? Are we excited about the day ahead? Wouldn't it be great if we woke up feeling alive?

Remember: passion gives you energy. No matter the industry or job title, if you find work that stems from your passion, you'll look forward to going to work, connecting more deeply with your colleagues, and, most importantly, enjoying a more powerful, purposeful life. In other words, find your passion and create a more awesome life.

Take the first step: Use your journal to note where your passion lives today. What can you do to light up that passion even more? Find a place to get quiet and limit external distractions and noises. (Where's your phone?) Listen to your heart, yourself, and your higher power. When we're quiet, God will show us what we're supposed to be doing and the actions we're supposed to take. Be aware of what you, God, or the universe is trying to tell you.

Let this calm, peaceful moment inspire your search for passion. Ask yourself questions and be honest with the answer:

- Do a freestyle writing exercise about the word *passion*.
- What are the roots of your passion? Where do you feel the happiest and most fulfilled? When do you feel the most energy?
- How do you put those things at the core of your life?
- What are your goals, and why do you care about them?
- What is your passion, and how can you pursue it?
- What lights you up or puts fire in your belly?

Now engage in a simple activity:

- Ask five friends or family members when they see you at your most passionate. Record the answers.
- Once you have their responses, reflect on what you think each answer means.

> **SAMPLE JOURNAL RESPONSE**
>
> So many times, while getting ready to author this book or during its actual creation, I have found that even if I am tired, it gives me energy, and I feel very purposeful. Writing has become something I do to provide peace, purpose, and power.
>
> The more time I get to be quiet and write, the better and simpler life becomes.

7

Confidence

"Feeling sure of yourself and your abilities."

As I mentioned in chapter two, I thought Bryson was the brokerage where I'd end my insurance career, but after about six years, I found it was no longer a good fit. Still, for months, I was in denial that I needed to change.

Sometimes, when we have tough issues to come to grips with, we hope that something will change overnight and we won't have to make that tough decision; it will fix itself. We won't have to make that decision; it will be made for us, and that hard, scary thing will disappear. Unfortunately, life doesn't work like that. We have to make challenging decisions and take steps to implement them. I had to do that when it was time to leave Bryson. But deep down, I wasn't confident I could make such a drastic change that late in my career. However, after I did the journaling exercise that day at the office, I could no longer ignore the fact that I had to make a move. The situation was not going to fix itself; I had to take some action. Still, I needed to determine where to turn or my next step. I was still determining how to move forward.

I was driving home from work one night, and my frustrations started rising. Typically, on my commute home, I'd listen to music or ruminate about the day, which I found a relaxing way to unwind. But on this particular drive, my anxiety was so high that I exclaimed aloud what I like to call "my very bold prayer": *God, I'm done. I can't do this anymore. I don't know what to do. I need to leave, but I need help figuring out my next steps. So please, I'm looking for a little direction here.* That was November 10, 2016. I'll never forget that drive home because it marked a significant turning point.

The next week, I stepped out. A thought sprang into my head: *call Steve Kearley*. I wasn't sure where that tiny voice came from or why it told me to call Steve, the owner of Benson Kearley IFG. However, I did hear one thing loud and clear—I was being asked to take confident steps forward. I decided, why not? Steve and I go back fifty years. We attended the same church and played hockey together in our younger years. We grew up together and went into the same business, but over time, our paths diverged. We hadn't spoken in probably twenty years, but something told me it was time for us to reconnect, even if he didn't have an opening at Benson. I had run into Steve at an insurance industry event earlier that year. Was that a chance meeting, or was that a meeting of destiny? I believe it was all part of my life's plan.

Steve and I set up lunch for the end of November. We had a wonderful time catching up over a beautiful meal. We reminisced about how I sold him his first car (a 1979 Buick Regal) and sang at his and his wife, Christine's wedding. At some point, I got down to business, told him I was interested in finding a new position, and asked him to keep me in mind if he heard anything. Unfortunately, there were no open positions at Benson, but Steve and I agreed to stay in touch. When I got home later that day, I felt more relaxed than I had in a long time. I had no idea what might happen, but I had taken a small but positive step.

Landing a job at Benson seemed like a shot in the dark in some ways, but I felt it had the potential to work out. I had no reason to believe that—the senior leadership at Benson was firmly entrenched—but I couldn't shake the feeling that something would open up that was just right for me.

After we rekindled our connection, Steve and I got together for lunch or dinner several times over the following months. My partner, Sara, always told me I was a different person after those meetings, that I was energetic, buoyant, and on fire. I had confidence that something was going to happen. It's that gut feeling again. I was leaning on my faith that something was going to work out. I took a step out, and that was what was needed. If you feel like you should do something, even if you don't know why, you do it. Faith is believing in something with no tangible evidence. But I also had to be patient and wait to see what unfolded.

During that time, I discovered a song that helped me figure out my next steps. I listened to it a hundred times during that long, brisk winter. The title is "Still" by Hillary Scott and The Scott Family. The song is about having faith that unseen things are happening in your favor, mountains are being moved, and waters are being parted. Listening to it, I knew I was supposed to have faith and confidence that my plans, dreams, and greatest desires would come together even if I didn't understand how. Faith gave me confidence, and confidence helped my faith grow. The two are intertwined.

I just needed to put myself out there and take the first step. The song encouraged me to do just that and say, "I trust you have a plan for me, and I'm just going to relax and let it unfold." I drew so much confidence from this song during that patient season. Another song on the same album also resonated with me. The title was "Thy Will." As I listened to both songs repeatedly, I reassured myself *that there was a plan here. I need to relax. It's under control.* There is a verse from the Bible I have held onto for a long time. It reminds us of who is in control: "For I know the plans . . . to prosper you and not to harm you, plans to give you hope and a future" Jeremiah 29:11 (NIV).

Winter eventually gave way to spring. In April, Steve called me, saying, "Our Vice President of Operations has decided to leave the insurance business, and we need somebody to take her spot." Naturally, I jumped at the chance. My faith and confidence had paid off. The divine plan was already in play; I just had to have *faith* that it existed and *trust that it would unfold.* For me, the relationship between faith and confidence is very tight. My faith gives me the confidence to step out and that I will be directed to the right place.

I never dreamed of being the Chief Operating Officer of a multimillion-dollar insurance brokerage, but I gradually built up my confidence and exit plan. First, I acknowledged that I had to make a change. Then I reached out to Steve. That all took confidence. Unfortunately, when problems or setbacks arise, it can suck the self-assurance right out of me. That's why I strive to build genuine, unshakable confidence over time. True faith is learning to accept what I can't change and take control of what I can. But to take that control and make those changes—I need *confidence*.

So, how can you find your confidence? Like everything else, it's a process. But this chapter will illuminate some of the best long-term ways to restore confidence.

Building Confidence

Confidence is one of my eight tenets because everyone struggles with having it, yet being successful without it is difficult. But having confidence doesn't come with the flick of a switch. Like the other tenets, learning confidence requires daily practice. If you write daily about where you are confident and where you lack confidence, you can take steps to improve. Knowing *what to* improve helps the process.

You can't take confidence for granted. Even if you're the COO of a major company, at some point, you will need more confidence. However, the perception is that those who sit at the top of the hierarchy always have unshakable confidence. Social media makes it seem like most people are out there living confident, happy lives when the truth is everybody has doubts and insecurities. It's time to stop comparing yourself to others and work on finding confidence within yourself. We spend so much time surfing and wasting time online. What value do these online platforms actually provide? I know there is some value, but we must watch our time. This is not the place to compare ourselves to everyone else online.

These are some of the distractions that we are bombarded with daily.

To have a successful life, we must feel good about where we are, believe we are accomplishing something, and have faith that we are heading in a positive direction. Each of us must define what success is. It is different for everyone. So much of that feeling good stems from confidence. If we have a negative self-image, we may still have some success, but we may not enjoy it. Confidence not only helps us be successful, but it helps us enjoy our success more. Confidence is key to creating more awesome in our lives, so here are a few ways to build it.

Consider Your Top Five

Jim Rohn says, "We are the average of the top five people we spend the most time with." Those top five people in our lives significantly influence who we become. In other words, hanging around five rock stars makes us more likely to become rock stars. If we hang around negative people, then we'll become negative. The moral of the story? Surrounding ourselves with the people who will enhance our lives is crucial.

The people around us can build up or tear down our confidence. If we hang out with negative people who don't share the same values, we must look honestly at ourselves and our relationships. The five most significant people in our lives substantially influence our life's direction.

Look at your life. Do you spend time with people who give you confidence? Or do you hang out with people who drain it? It would be best to stay vigilant about what goes into our hearts and minds. I talked earlier about being that reservoir. If you spend time with people who constantly drain you, you must find somewhere else to get filled up again. Your Top Five people cannot be the ones who drain you. Is this selfish? No, it's protecting what's most important to your future and your goals.

Protecting ourselves also needs to apply to family, and that's challenging for some of us. I hear all the time from people that a certain family member sucks the life out of them. Just because someone is family, however, they do not have a special right to chip away at your confidence.

If you have family members in your Top Five who negatively impact you, there are two ways to pull back respectfully. The first is to have a direct conversation about the issue. Yes, it will probably be uncomfortable but think about the alternative: you continue to get dragged down by this relationship. If you want to go this route, clearly state that you're talking about their behaviour or attitude, not them. If you're unsure what to say, keep it simple and tell your relative, "I need a little distance here, so you may not hear from me as often."

The second way is to discreetly reduce your exposure to this individual or group. If you go this route, it's good to make a plan and make a real commitment to execute that plan. For example, a few of my friends gather every Thursday night for a drink, but lately, the conversation has turned negative. You might start going every other Thursday night for a while. Then, cut back to once a month. A simple plan will help you quietly and respectfully take control of the five people you spend the most time with.

Over the years, I've found different ways to withdraw from harmful relationships respectfully. Just because someone is close to me doesn't mean they have the right to damage my sense of self-worth. The same goes for my friends, coworkers, and loved ones. I invest most of my time and energy in the folks who lift me and minimize my time with the rest.

Get Prepared

Growing up, I sang in the church and choirs, quartets, trios, and duets; I even did some solo work. I even sang in a few groups that travelled around Ontario on the weekends, singing at churches. Whether doing a solo or performing as part of a choir, I must rehearse. If I don't rehearse, it will sound terrible, and my message won't come across. Ask anyone who's performed in front of a crowd: singing unprepared is a disaster. But the song will turn out beautifully when I prepare, learn all the parts, and rehearse them well. That practice and preparation gave me the confidence to go on stage. My message is received clearly with no distractions.

We feel surer of ourselves when we know what we're doing. I tell our sales department this all the time. Insurance is quite a technical field, and good sales representatives must have precise, prepared knowledge. Despite that, I sometimes see sales reps attend a client meeting unprepared. They should have planned an agenda or prepared for their client's questions. It always turns out to be a disaster. It makes the client lose confidence in the sales rep, and the sales rep loses confidence in him or herself.

About twenty years ago, I started attending every client meeting with an agenda. During my long life in sales, preparation gave me confidence. It also demonstrated to my clients that I cared enough to prepare. And by preparing for our meeting, I added value to their business, life, and day.

Preparation gives us the confidence to proceed with *whatever* we're doing. I've brought that knack for practice to my leadership role at Benson. I prepare for the Friday team huddles by creating an outline to understand how the huddle might flow. I don't always follow my outline because I also like to allow spontaneity and reading the room, but because I'm prepared, I have options. I can stick to the script or go with the flow, but I have something to work with. I show our team I value their time by making our huddles meaningful. The most important thing is knowing there's an order, a sequence, and a reason for being there.

Preparation has been a useful skill my entire life. And it's filled me with the confidence to sing in a choir, meet my clients, and lead the team. Do you see how preparation can help you build your confidence? Let's say you have a meeting next week, and you're having lunch with a prospect for the first time. What can you do to prepare? Research the person on LinkedIn, and research the company online. Prepare an agenda for the information you want to secure. Have a brainstorming session and use your journal to jot down thoughts, ideas, and questions. If you have a plan, you can have confidence.

Stay Positive

Confidence puts a spring in our step because *real* confidence—not arrogance or ego—has a positive energy. If we're constantly focused on the negative, we're simply not going to have that same spring in our step. Worry will take our attitude down. The problem is that it is human nature to focus on the negative. If twenty wonderful things happen in a day, but one terrible thing happens too, we usually end up hyper-focused on that one awful thing. It keeps us up at night. Over time, our tendency to focus on the negative depletes our confidence. So, how do we combat this?

First, remember that the positives outnumber the negatives on any given day. Still, like everything else in this book, you must take a moment to reflect intentionally upon that positivity. That's why I dedicate time to journaling about the good things that have happened during the week. Every Friday, I write up a simple list of positives. This list could include a great phone call with a client, an enjoyable conversation with a team member, or a client meeting that went well. That way, before I walk out of the office to head into my weekend, my mind isn't focused on the one thing that's still a mess. Maybe I made a mistake or am still trying to problem-solve for a client—sure, I need to think about those things to fix them, but they shouldn't dominate my headspace. Those negatives were *part* of my week, but not *all* of it. So, I try to balance out my perspective by giving more attention to the positive.

We must remind our brains to focus on the good things in our lives. So that's why I make that positivity list exercise a habit, something other than what I do here or there when I have the time. I've done this for years, and I only allow myself to skip this exercise during the holidays when my schedule gets thrown off. In 2021, my mom fell ill, and I had to force myself to make that weekly list of positives. I skipped more weeks than usual. Then, in October of 2021, my mother passed away, and I didn't feel like making a list at all. But when the new year came, I realized something: my positive outlook had dwindled and had taken my confidence with it. It had been a tough year, and it made sense, but this was not where my head could or should stay. I had to find myself again.

I knew slipping into unhealthy habits and out of a confident mindset was not what my mom would have wanted. I returned to my Strategic Coach Goal Sheet, which I discussed in chapter two, and set a firm goal to return to my Friday ritual. My passion for being positive helped me get back on track. Fortunately, I was successful in meeting my goal. I was focused on returning to a more positive frame of mind. Thank goodness for that because what we focus on *grows*. After a hard year, I needed my positive mindset and confidence to succeed. I kept writing that positivity list through the first, second, third, and fourth quarters. I had completed my goal; my Friday positivity exercise was back to being a habit. I could tell the difference, too, because, by the end of 2022, I was feeling more upbeat and surer about my life, which restored my confidence.

When you have a positive habit and stop for any reason, it will negatively impact you. If I set out to go to the gym twice a week when I go, I feel great—every single time. But if I choose not to go, two things happen: first, I feel bad for missing my work out and beat myself up for not being more committed, and second, my health deteriorates. Breaking one good habit causes two negative things.

Call to Create Awesome: Confidence

Over the next thirty days, do the following journal prompts and exercises to boost your confidence.

Take the first step: Use your journal to note acts of giving or receiving you engage in. Find a place to get quiet and limit external distractions and noises. (Phone . . . lose it, just for a few minutes. You will survive!) Listen to your heart, yourself, and your higher power. When we're quiet, God will show us what we're supposed to be doing and the actions we're supposed to take. Be aware of what you, God, or the universe is trying to tell you.

Let this calm, peaceful moment inspire your thoughts on confidence. Ask yourself questions and be honest with the answer:

- Do a freestyle writing exercise on the word *confidence*.
- When do you have the most confidence?
- What and who gives you confidence?
- What depletes your confidence?

- What habits can you add to your life to help your confidence grow?

Take an Inventory of Your Top Five

- Identify the Top Five people in your life.

    - Who do you spend the most time with?
    - Who has the most influence on your behaviour?
    - Who do you look to for advice?

- Then, do a little bit of inventory.

    - Does each person in your Top Five have a more negative or positive influence on your life? Why are those people with whom you spend the most time?
    - Do you need to make any changes? If so, what do you need to change? How can you change it respectfully? Do you have to cut out the relationship or reduce exposure? And even more important, how can you spend more time with the positive influences in your life?

Make a Positivity List

- Set aside time at the end of your week or over the weekend to list all the good things that happened the week before.

- Observe and record how this list impacts your confidence.

Consider the Connection Between Passion and Confidence

In the chapter on passion, we discussed how when you're feeling passionate, you have confidence because you're doing exactly what you're supposed to be doing. Passion and confidence work together hand in hand. If you're confident doing something, it's likely because you have a passion for it, and vice versa.

- Consider the link between passion and confidence in your life. How are they connected to you?

- Do you feel more confident when you do what you're passionate about?

- Identify some things that help you be more confident. How can you do more of those things in your life?

I hope this chapter has given you the confidence to know who you are hanging out with and what impact they have on your life, positive or negative.

SAMPLE JOURNAL RESPONSE

I have a very small group of people I connect with. The size of my group has never been large; however, over the years, it has become smaller by choice. I only need or want a few connections. What I want and strive for are just the ones that make me a better person.

8

Legacy

"Something that is passed on."

For most of my life, I didn't think much about leaving a legacy. We don't give legacy much thought in our 20s, 30s, or 40s. We are busy building our lives, not thinking about what seems to be something in the distant future. That changed the day I attended a memorial service for Joan Francolini—Mrs. F, as I referred to her. Joan was Sara's mother, and though she was in my life briefly, she left a very big impression.

What struck me most was Mrs. F, who passed away at eighty and had so much energy, vitality, and an amazing future ahead until the last couple of years. Eighty did not seem like it should have been the end for her. She had spent nearly thirty years focused on motherhood and then enjoyed a personal and professional renaissance in the last few decades of her life. She had six children, and her husband travelled for work, so raising her family occupied most of her adult life. But Joan began a second life once the kids were grown and married. She served on local committees and joined various boards. She was an incredible speaker who was blessed with business and leadership savvy. Joan's contributions as a board member have helped shape her home city of London, Ontario, for over thirty years. She was a member of the London Community Foundation, YMCA, United Way of London, and Middlesex, among many others. She enjoyed many distinctions, including the Order of Ontario and the Dr. Ivan Smith Alumni Award of Merit, the highest honour a Western University graduate can receive. She was heavily involved in her alma mater, Brescia University College, and in February 2013, was named Brescia's *first* chancellor. Joan and her husband, Geno, were generous in their contributions to the school. They were known for quietly paying for struggling students' tuition or caring for Brescia's community members in unexpected ways.

During Mrs. F's memorial service, I realized that the most incredible opportunities and accomplishments sometimes happen later in life. Of course, raising six great kids was an accomplishment in and of itself, but Joan didn't leave it at that. She was a compassionate leader who strived to do more for her community, and she succeeded in a short amount of time.

Listening to the service unfold, I started reflecting upon my life and legacy. At that time, I couldn't even answer what kind of legacy I wanted to leave, let alone how I'd do it. I was already in my mid-fifties and believed it was too late to leave a positive legacy. But hearing story after story about Mrs. F made me realize I still had plenty of time.

After that, legacy became an important part of my journaling practice. Thinking and writing about my legacy helped me answer life's big questions: *Why was I born? And what am I supposed to accomplish while I'm here?*

Since then, I've come to appreciate that age is irrelevant to legacy; you're never too old or too young to be thinking about it. Like me, at that time, so many people believed creating a legacy had already passed them by, but Mrs. F's legacy taught me that a single person could make a significant impact over time. Still, others believe that creating a legacy is something we wait to do once we get old. But I want to emphasize that legacy is also a young person's game. The sooner we start thinking about our legacy, the sooner we engage in an intentional life.

We shouldn't take our time on Earth for granted. There are no guarantees about how long we'll be here. Since we don't know how much time we have and what we're capable of with the time given, we might start thinking about our legacy today.

This chapter will outline the best way to start doing so and help you move forward with a legacy that feels authentic to you.

Honouring Generational Legacies

I always wanted to author a book, but it seemed like a flight of fancy. However, over time, I knew this had to be written. I wanted to make a difference, and I saw authoring a book as a way to have my message of creating awesome out there long after I am gone. But it also honours the legacy of those who have come before me, particularly my mother. After all, I have so much of my mom in me. Watching how she lived in such a meaningful and giving way plays out in my life today. My mom was a funny, generous, spiritual, and kind human being. She inspires me and the legacy I want to leave, and I believe that long after I'm gone, my legacy will influence others similarly.

I've mentioned how pivotal music has created awesome in my life. After my mom passed away, I frequently played the song "Scars in Heaven" by Casting Crowns. My favourite lyric is, "The better parts of you live on in me." That's what I like to believe about legacy—that the better parts of me came from my mom, and those are the parts that I want to grow and then pass on. I see my mom, Pat Bundock, alive and well in my daughter, son-in-law, grandchildren, and great-grandchildren. This book is about my legacy and honouring those who came before me and those who come after. In this case, what I've learned over the years from mom, who remains the single biggest influence in my life, and my grandchildren, who give me purpose every day.

Legacy Can Be Simple

My dad's name was Murray, and back in the 1980s, when the Ontario Government started allowing personalized license plates, he was among the first to get one. Dad got the plate MUZZ because that was his nickname. He used to sign *everything* Muzz, even business letters. My father had that license plate on his car until he passed away in 2000, and I came to identify his name and that license plate closely with him.

One day, shortly after my dad passed, my mom and I were wrapping up his estate. She asked me, "So what do you want to do with that plate?" I had only considered that question once my mother asked, but letting the license plate go seemed wrong. How could the MUZZ not be driving around out there? I told my mom that the license plate had become integral to our family and that we should keep it. After that conversation, my mom signed the license plate over to me, and I proudly showcased MUZZ on the back of my car for over twenty years.

But the legend of MUZZ doesn't end there. My nephew Jake was close to my dad and always said, "If you ever want to part with that license plate, I will take it over." In the back of my mind, I knew I'd pass it down to Jake someday, but I never found the right moment, so I just let the thought dance around in my subconscious. But then, in September 2021, Jake and his wife, Ashleigh, had a baby boy. They named him Oliver Murray Martin Bundock—the Murray, of course, in honour of my dad.

A couple of weeks after Oliver Murray was born, I decided it was appropriate to give Jake the plate. I went to the Ministry of Transportation and signed the ownership papers over. I also got an old copy of the plate refinished and framed so that Jake could hang it in Oliver's nursery. Before I was able to give Jake this gift, my mom passed away. I presented Jake with papers for the official license plate and the framed Muzz plate the day before my mother's funeral. The emotions running through the room that afternoon were extraordinary. Jake burst into tears, and we shared a long hug.

My dad had that plate for twenty years, I had it for another twenty years, and I expect Jake will have it for twenty years on top of that. Maybe little Oliver Murray will have it for twenty years after that. With any luck, MUZZ will live on forever. Regardless, my dad, mom, Jake, Oliver, and I created awesome through legacy.

Call to Create Awesome: Legacy

For most of this book, we've discussed creating an intentional life. Now, it's time to create an intentional legacy. What will live on long after I am gone?

At Mrs. F's memorial service, I understood that my legacy would look different than hers because no two legacies are alike. So, while journaling, I frequently ask myself, "What will my legacy be?" Asking that question urges me to think more deeply about where I came from and what I want to leave behind. Legacy is personal, and it should be. The legacy you leave behind should be about what matters to you. There are no rules.

It can be hard to define legacy because there is no exact way to prepare to leave it. That's part of the discovery process, and that's why journaling can be a valuable tool for self-exploration.

Take the first step: Use your journal to note acts of giving or receiving you engage in. Find a place to get quiet and limit external distractions and noises. (I don't have to remind you to lose the phone again, do I?) Listen to your heart, yourself, and your higher power. When we're quiet, God will show us what we're supposed to be doing and the actions we're supposed to take. Be aware of what you, God, or the universe is trying to tell you.

The following prompts and exercises will help you reflect on your legacy.

- What would you like to say at your memorial service? Write down your thoughts in the third person, as if a close friend, family member, or colleague were speaking about you.
- What actions must you take for those words to be said?
- What things do you need to change to make those actions happen?

Create Legacy Habits

Unlike the other seven tenets, you don't have to consider legacy daily. Still, it is part of the big picture, and I encourage you to journal about your legacy regardless—your habits, like your goals, kindness, and giving, often become part of your legacy.

- Do a freestyle writing exercise on the word *legacy*.
- How will the other habits in this book help you build your legacy?
- What habits, in particular, make you feel most connected to your legacy?

Insert three questions about how I want to be remembered.

I've always wanted to have a positive impact, and that desire came from watching my mother and folks like the Crawfords and Mrs. F. They all enjoyed paving different paths. I want to honour their legacy while shaping my own. My approach is about creating awesome for the people around me and helping them create awesome in their lives. It's worthwhile to strive for the best possible life and experience the joy of self-discovery. And so that's the legacy I want to leave.

This book can do the same for those around me.

> **SAMPLE JOURNAL RESPONSE**
>
> Authoring this book has become a huge part of what I hope will be a positive and lasting legacy. My daughter or grandkids may carry the Create Awesome torch for a time. Perhaps years from now, someone will find this book on Amazon or some other website, and it might just make a difference. My goal would be to make an impact for years to come.

Conclusion

A few days ago, I did my morning ritual and headed to a coffee shop to work on the conclusion of this book and do a little journaling if I had time. While there, I noticed that one of the baristas was sitting at the counter writing. I drank my coffee, finished my pages, and packed up for the day. On my way out, I paused and asked her, "Are you journaling?"

She perked up and replied, "Yes, I am. But I'm all over the place today, so I'm just putting pen and paper and letting my mind go where it wants to go."

Now, it was my turn to perk up. I showed her my journal and explained how I use certain words and prompts to inspire my daily writing habit. The barista mentioned how she doesn't keep a special journal, but she's been wanting to. Then, she commented on how she always wanted a dedicated journal and a Montblanc pen.

Unbelievably, I had a Montblanc pen in my briefcase. It was unused for five years because it didn't fit my grip. So, I conceived a plan. The next day, I returned for my usual morning ritual, but I didn't come empty-handed: I brought her one of my special leatherbound journals with the words *Create Awesome* embossed on the cover. As with the books I keep on my Giving Shelf, I also keep a stack of these journals to pass them out to those who might appreciate them.

I gave her the journal and shared my eight tenets with her. Then, I gave her the pen. I told her that while I appreciated the craftsmanship of a Montblanc, it wasn't a good fit for me, so I wanted to pass it on to her. She was over the moon.

I have so many stories that I was connecting over journaling, which has impacted someone's life. There was a month or two when I kept running into the same customer while visiting one of my favourite coffee shops. While I would journal, he would write and work on his laptop. He and I were usually the only ones there, so he must have noticed the car out front was mine. My licence plate is CRE8AWSM, and one day, he commented that he thought it was a great phrase. I was delighted and decided to bring him one of my Create Awesome journals as a token of appreciation. Unfortunately, I forgot to pack it on my way out the door. One day, as I was getting my journal and pens from my briefcase in my car's trunk, I noticed a few journals I hadn't seen before. I grabbed one to bring inside for him, thrilled it finally worked out, only to find out he wasn't inside. I settled into my seat, ready to start writing. Minutes later, he walked in.

After he ordered his latte and got situated, I wandered over with my modest gift. I explained how my journaling practice and favourite slogan, Create Awesome, were part of my life mission—and the inspiration for my plate. He thanked me and asked if I would sign it, which made my day. A few minutes later, he returned to where I was sitting and thanked me again. He told me it was his birthday and that the journal improved his day.

For a month, I had forgotten to take a journal to him, and the one day I remembered was his birthday. What a great—and unexpected—way to create awesome.

These stories encapsulate everything in this book: giving, kindness, passion, journaling, keeping habits, and all the rest. Now it's your time to create awesome *your* way.

A Short Compendium of Awesome

So, how can you start creating awesome your way? Review each chapter's summary and decide which word speaks to you. Then, get journaling! It takes some time, but as you get into the routine, things you had not given much thought to before will suddenly come alive and into sharp focus.

Chapter 1: Faith

Faith is an invisible force that lives in the heart and the soul. Calling upon faith shores up your confidence so you can move through challenges, great and small. Pinning your hopes and dreams on something invisible is no small task, but if you let things flow through faith, I promise it will change your life.

Chapter 2: Goals

You may have an underlying sense that you can improve your life, but you might need help knowing where to start. You need to set intentional, mindful, personal goals. You can only understand how to improve the quality of your life if you name the things that will do just that.

Chapter 3: Giving

Giving doesn't cost you anything; it often brings you more than you give. You must think past your needs occasionally and share your gifts with others.

Chapter 4: Kindness

It's vital to your well-being to cultivate and increase your capacity for kindness. Protecting yourself from hostile environments and bad headspaces is equally important to be kinder to yourself and those around you.

Chapter 5: Gratitude

Regardless of your situation, there's always something to be thankful for. Gratitude must become a regular practice so you can see the vast abundance surrounding you.

Chapter 6: Passion

People always think you either have a passion or you don't. It is inside you; you must take the time to locate it and nurture it. You must seek your passion—not the other way around. And it's worth going on the hunt because passion gives you energy and an abundant, fulfilled life.

Chapter 7: Confidence

When problems or setbacks arise, they can suck the confidence out of you. Real confidence is learning to accept what you can't change and take control of what you can. To do that, you need confidence in yourself.

Chapter 8: Legacy

Creating a lasting legacy fills your life with purpose, but so many people have the misconception that creating a legacy is something made when you get old. Others think creating their legacy has already passed them by. Neither is true. Start creating your legacy now.

Committing to Awesome

I hope this book inspired you to actively engage in the eight tenets, use the exercises, and commit to creating a habit of quiet reflection. If so, you've taken critical steps to improve your life. Some changes may be gradual, while others are more noticeable, but every effort will be meaningful and intentional.

But my greatest hope is that you find the journey to awesome is accessible to you. Make this process your own. What does journaling mean to you? What does creating awesome mean to you?

This is about something other than how I have created the secret to success. Yes, I have a few ingredients that work well: clearing distractions, sitting in quiet reflection, and writing down what comes up. But feel free to use my ingredients to make your own recipe.

If by the time you've reached this conclusion, you've bought a journal and jotted a few things down, that is a success story. When I hand out my Create Awesome leatherbound journals, my greatest joy is getting an email a month later that says, "Hey

Doug, thanks for the journal. I use it every day. I've been wanting to do this for a long time." For me, that's enough. I don't ask, "What are you getting out of it? What's your next goal? What's changed since you started writing in it?" That's for them to decide. And the same goes for you.

This is your journey. You decide how it unfolds.

Reasons to Journal

Clarity and Mental Focus: Journaling helps organize your thoughts and clarify your ideas. It enhances mental focus by providing a dedicated space to explore and articulate your goals, aspirations, and plans.

Creative Exploration: Journaling encourages creativity and imagination. It allows you to explore new ideas, experiment with different writing styles, and tap into your creative potential.

Emotional Release: Writing your thoughts and feelings in a journal can be therapeutic. It allows you to express and release pent-up emotions, reducing stress and promoting emotional well-being.

Gratitude and Appreciation: Keeping a gratitude journal helps cultivate a positive mindset and appreciation for the present moment. It lets you focus on your gratitude, fostering a sense of contentment and well-being.

Memory Enhancement: Regular journaling can improve memory and cognitive function. When you write about your experiences, you reinforce the neural connections associated with those memories, making them easier to recall in the future.

Personal Growth and Development: Journaling promotes personal growth by fostering self-awareness, self-discovery, and self-improvement. It allows you to track your progress, identify patterns, and set goals for personal development

Problem Solving: Writing about challenges and dilemmas in your journal can help you analyze them objectively. It enables you to brainstorm solutions, evaluate different perspectives, and gain new insights into potential resolutions.

Self-Reflection: Journaling provides a space for self-reflection, allowing you to gain deeper insights into your thoughts, emotions, and experiences. It helps you better understand yourself and your reactions to various situations.

Stress Reduction: Writing in a journal can be calming and soothing. It helps alleviate stress by providing an outlet for worries, anxieties, and frustrations, ultimately leading to greater inner peace.

CREATE AWESOME

JUST FOR TODAY

Just for today: I WILL FOCUS ON MY FAITH

Just for today: I WILL FOCUS ON THESE 8 CREATE AWESOME WORDS

Just for today: I WILL DEVELOP AND CREATE MEANINGFUL GOALS

Just for today: I WILL SPEND TIME WORKING ON MY FINANCES

Just for today: I WILL SPEND 10 MINUTES BEING QUIET

Just for today: I WILL THINK OF WAYS TO BE KIND

Just for today: I WILL WRITE DOWN THREE REASONS I AM GRATEFUL

Just for today: I WILL THINK ABOUT THINGS THAT GIVE ME ENERGY

Just for today: I WILL DO ONE THING THAT GIVES ME CONFIDENCE

Just for today: I WILL PLAN FOR AND MODEL GENEROSITY

Just for today: I WILL SEEK AND EXPERIENCE IMPROVEMENTS

Just for today: I WILL THINK OF WHAT MY LEGACY WILL BE

JUST FOR TODAY . . . I WILL ACT ON THESE DECISIONS AND PRACTISE THESE DISCIPLINES,

AND

I WILL SEE THE COMPOUNDING RESULTS OF A DAY LIVED WELL.

Create Awesome

In the realm of dreams and destiny's embrace, a tapestry woven with threads of grace. Faith, the guiding light that ignites the soul, urges us toward our truest goal.

With fervent passion and unrelenting might, we chase aspirations that set hearts alight. For within us lies a fire that burns bright, igniting our ambitions and reaching for new heights.

Kindness is the currency we freely bestow. In every interaction, let compassion and empathy flow. Give of ourselves, extend a hand, and create waves of love across the land.

Gratitude is a balm for the spirit's ache, a humble acknowledgement of what we race. Daily blessings are often invisible until we search.

In giving, we are enriched, and blessings are abundant. To give of ourselves is soothing to the soul.

Confidence is a beacon through stormy seas, empowering us to conquer what may displease. With an unwavering belief in our might, we conquer obstacles unyielding in our fight.

As we march forward, leaving footprints in time, we build a legacy, a monument so sublime. Through acts of greatness, big and small, we craft an awesome tapestry that enthralls.

So let us unite with these words in our creed: Embrace our purpose, and let our hearts take the lead. We strive with faith, goals, giving, and kindness, leaving behind a legacy that will forever reside.

In this grand tapestry, we all play a part, and each thread of awesomeness we impart will weave a narrative that inspires and uplifts, a masterpiece of humanity, a treasure that never drifts.

About the Author

Drawing from over forty-eight years of business experience, Douglas Bundock guides readers in his work, *Create Awesome: Journaling Your Way to an Intentional Life*, helping them gain control over their journey towards intentional living. He brings a deep understanding of leadership and life's challenges, sharing the practical insights and tools he's learned along the way so that he can help others find their true purpose and create awesome in their lives.

Douglas lives in Markham, Ontario, with his spouse, Sara. He is a licensed insurance broker in Ontario through RIBO and is certified by the John Maxwell Organization for speaking and coaching. He also holds a Risk Management Designation (CRM) in Ontario. When he's not writing, Douglas enjoys working in his yard, woodworking, often giving new life to old furniture and window frames. He also loves cycling and has completed the Ride to Conquer Cancer multiple times.

www.ingramcontent.com/pod-product-compliance
Lightning Source LLC
Jackson TN
JSHW080137301224
76220JS00001B/2